"Bill Heatley mixes delightful b[...] reflection in constructing this r[...] a buoyancy to the prose that infuses the reader with hope that work matters—that it is an opportunity rather than a life sentence."

—RANDY KILGORE, MDiv, workplace chaplain; author of *Made to Matter*

"When Bill Heatley says, 'Doing my job within God's kingdom is the most exciting and challenging experience I know,' this is not the cheap hype of a PR man. It took the experience of losing everything to teach Bill the price of pursuing success at the expense of goodness. *The Gift of Work* introduces us to a different way of working. Honest, inspiring, and well worth reading."

—ALISTAIR MACKENZIE, director, Faith At Work (New Zealand); author of *Ethics for the Marketplace, SoulPurpose,* and *Where's God on Monday?*

"Bill Heatley puts working clothes on discipleship and spiritual disciplines in a way that stimulates personal and cultural transformation. His enlightening work sees corporate profits and products as important results of a positive, caring corporate culture sustained by people doing the right things. He brings us a vocabulary to use in carrying Christ into the center of a loving community at work and in every sphere of influence."

—MERRILL J. OSTER, international financial publisher; author; entrepreneur

"This is a sensitive, far-ranging discussion of the personal challenges and opportunities for workers to find God's inspired purposes in their work linked to wider arenas of their lives. From a personal and honest declaration of the reality of workplaces as he has experienced them, Heatley details how the discipline of spending time with God and the Word offers the strength to live in fulfillment in work. If employers, management, and workers were prepared to implement Bill Heatley's recommendations, policies, and programs, Christian relationships and creativity would transform society's productivity and stability."

—CARA BEED, CLIVE BEED, (Cara) MEd Sociology lecturer and Graduate Advisor, Australian Catholic University (retired); (Clive) PhD Economics Senior lecturer, University of Melbourne (retired)

"Bill Heatley's *The Gift of Work* is a gift itself. It is informed by a solid grasp of Scripture, years of business experience, and time in the school of hard knocks. Heatley shares the insights of the spiritual masters, mediated often by his mentor Dallas Willard and applied using his own savvy experience, to produce a user-friendly road map to the spirituality of work. Highly commended to those wanting to bridge the gap between their faith and work."

—REVEREND DR. GORDON PREECE, executive director, Urban Seed, Melbourne; author of *Changing Work Values*

"Bill Heatley makes an insightful and much-needed contribution to the crucial but often neglected theme of a Christian spirituality of work. In this book, both mission and discipleship come together to show how the Christian life can become an all-day-and-every-day adventure rather than simply a Sunday and spare-time pursuit."

—DARRELL COSDEN, PhD, associate professor of theology, Judson University; author of *A Theology of Work*

SPIRITUAL DISCIPLINES FOR
THE WORKPLACE

THE GIFT OF
WORK

BILL HEATLEY

FOREWORD BY DALLAS WILLARD

Featuring the Message "How God Is in Business"
by Dallas Willard

NAVPRESS

NavPress is the publishing ministry of The Navigators, an international Christian organization and leader in personal spiritual development. NavPress is committed to helping people grow spiritually and enjoy lives of meaning and hope through personal and group resources that are biblically rooted, culturally relevant, and highly practical.

**For a free catalog go to www.NavPress.com
or call 1.800.366.7788 in the United States or 1.800.839.4769 in Canada.**

ISBN-13: 978-1-60006-134-9
ISBN-10: 1-60006-134-6

Cover design by The DesignWorks Group, Jason Gabbert, www.thedesignworksgroup.com
Cover images from Photos.com and Shutterstock

Some of the anecdotal illustrations in this book are true to life and are included with the permission of the persons involved. All other illustrations are composites of real situations, and any resemblance to people living or dead is coincidental.

Unless otherwise identified, all Scripture quotations in this publication are taken from the HOLY BIBLE: NEW INTERNATIONAL VERSION® (NIV®). Copyright © 1973, 1978, 1984 by International Bible Society. Used by permission of Zondervan Publishing House. All rights reserved. Other versions used include: the *New American Standard Bible* (NASB), © The Lockman Foundation 1960, 1962, 1963, 1968, 1971, 1972, 1973, 1975, 1977, 1995; and the *King James Version* (KJV).

Library of Congress Cataloging-in-Publication Data

Heatley, Bill, 1958-
  The gift of work : spiritual disciplines for the workplace / Bill
Heatley ; featuring the message "How God is in business" by Dallas
Willard.
     p. cm.
  Includes bibliographical references.
  ISBN-13: 978-1-60006-134-9
  ISBN-10: 1-60006-134-6
  1. Work--Religious aspects--Christianity. I. Title.
  BT738.5.H43 2008
  248.8'8--dc22
                         2008006220

Printed in the United States of America

1 2 3 4 5 6 7 8 / 11 10 09 08

In gratitude I dedicate this book to the hard-working men and women whose dedication and devotion to their jobs ensure the great bounty of our nation. May you find within these pages the light of God's love in His creation of work and the blessing that it richly extends to all His children. May this knowledge lighten your burden, provide rest for your soul, and fill your heart with joy in the shadow of His wings.

3/9/12

Dana,
I hope this book will be a blessing to you as you shine light w/ your fellow associates. We studied this book at our church and actually brought Bill (author) in for the teaching. 3 days of being a blessing to me. Art
Jer 29:11

CONTENTS

ACKNOWLEDGMENTS

My heartfelt gratitude to . . .

My dad, who taught me fortitude and duty in the face of adversity.

My wife, Becky, who taught me love.

Dallas Willard, for his boundless wisdom, generosity, and love of Jesus.

My family and friends, who have steadfastly supported my efforts.

My children, who remind me of what's really important.

FOREWORD

We human beings are situated in a world structured by small and large systems of hidden powers. On the physical side, the discovery of the wheel and the lever, and the harnessing of heat (fire, steam, internal combustion engines), electricity, and the atom are all illustrations of the unfolding destiny of humanity upon the earth. That destiny is, in biblical language, to "have dominion" (Genesis 1:26, KJV). That is, we are to be responsible for the earth and life upon it. Human inventions or discoveries are all related, in straightforward ways, to work. Work is the production of value by the actions of our thoughts and bodily efforts upon available resources.

What's more, work is a good thing, and it is a natural disposition of human beings from early childhood on. Work is simply human creativity. It is a special type of causation through which goodness and blessing can be promoted in our surroundings.

Except in the rare desert island kinds of cases, the values produced by work and the particular activities involved in work are social or communal in nature. They are strictly inconceivable, except in a communal setting, from the family on up. They depend upon others for their existence, and they are for the benefit of others as well as of the individual worker. This too is a good thing and part of God's arrangement for the virtue and prospering of human beings. Without a division of labor and suitable human relationships in community, human life can barely rise above the level of animals. So the great question is this: What is the resource that will enable human beings, developing the powers of nature, to live in a community where there is dignity, love, and provision for everyone?

We know very well some of the human answers to this vital question, and we have the bitter experience of their failures. The modern answers all focus upon the matter of ownership. That is, upon the question of who shall have the right to say what will be done with the resources. One says that the state or government should own the means (including money and human labor) by which goods are produced. That is socialism. (But the state turns out in practice just to be certain people, who may be neither wise nor competent nor good.) Communism says that no one should own those means of production. (But then it turns out that certain people do, for all practical purposes—regardless of the official arrangement.) Unrestrained capitalism says that enterprising individuals should own them, catch as catch can in fair competition. (But then *fair* gets defined by those who have the goods.)

None of these answers, we should now know, provides a moral solution to the human problems posed by work. In simple terms, this is because none of them deals with the fine texture of human motivation, with what men and women care about and live for. They are a form of the proverbial brain surgery with a meat cleaver. The popular theories of human action now taught in our best schools of management do little better.

Bill Heatley's book addresses this fundamental problem of finding appropriate community-in-work for human beings. That community is the resource without which all other resources languish or become dangerous. He addresses that problem at the level where work is done in a world not really structured around doing what is good and right, but around doing it *my* way and for *my* benefit. That is the level of the job. (Spelled, incidentally, just like the name of the all-time leader in suffering, Job. What a coincidence!) The solution Bill brings forward is that of Jesus Christ and His followers. It is the recognition of and intelligent reliance upon the community (kingdom, family) of God. That community is already there at your job, waiting to turn it back into rich and rewarding and meaningful work, creativity, shared production of goods to be shared. You don't make God's community, of course—you receive it, by counting on it and acting with it.

The accessibility of life in the community of God to every person was the message of Jesus, in His words and in His deeds. Everything else fits into that: forgiveness of sins, redemption from sin, transformation of character into "righteousness, peace and joy in the Holy Spirit" (Romans 14:17), transformation of society, and the development of history into everlasting life. In His efforts to help those around Him understand the message and reality of the community of God, Jesus on one occasion remarked that the community of God is not recognized by eyesight. It isn't something localizable in the world, like a human social group, a government (buildings), or an army. Rather, He said, it is already there, "in your midst" (Luke 17:21, NASB). That is to say, it is already where you are, wherever that may be, right now.

Now that was not a new thing in the time of Jesus, though it was for Him alone to manifest and to be its full meaning. In Deuteronomy, we read that God's Word and doing what He wants and supports "is not too difficult for you, nor is it out of reach. It is not in heaven, that you should say, 'Who will go up to heaven for us to get it for us and make us hear it, that we may observe [do] it?' Nor is it beyond the sea. . . . But the word is very near you, in your mouth and in your heart, that you may observe [do] it" (30:11-14, NASB). The twenty-third psalm is a poetic celebration of this life in "the everlasting arms" (Deuteronomy 33:27).

Paul, taught by Christ Himself, reclaims and enlarges this vision of our life in God (see Romans 10:8). He tells his Philippian friends:

"Our citizenship" (πολίτευμα)—our socioeconomic order, if you wish, or our commonwealth—"is in heaven" (Philippians 3:20). That means it is right around us ("in our midst"), not something far away and at some later time. We are now, as disciples of Jesus, members of a divine community that, when we seek it, we find with us in our job and throughout life, and thereby we turn all that we do into work for and under God. Thus, Paul advises: "Whatever you do, do your work heartily"—literally, "from the soul"—"as for the Lord rather than for men, knowing that from the Lord you will receive the reward of the inheritance. It is the Lord Christ whom you serve" (Colossians 3:23-24, NASB). We are not to try to look good (do "eyeservice"), as men-pleasers, but on our job we simply do "the will of God from the heart" (Ephesians 6:6, NASB).

Now this book tells us exactly how to do this. Intelligent, well-informed, and biblical to the core, it is intensely focused upon the real-life context of the job: on what really goes on there, and how, for our part, we can turn it into divine work. In this respect the author is telling us how to live a life that is spiritual throughout, full of meaning, strength, and joy. He thus stands in the solid tradition of Christian teaching throughout the ages. He does so with the freshness of personal experience and the forcefulness of careful thought.

Phillips Brooks was a great American pastor and teacher of a century ago. He was for a long time the pastor of one of the greatest churches in the United States, and sometimes the Anglican bishop of Massachusetts; but he was also a man of national prominence and influence. In his sermon, "Best Methods of Promoting Spiritual Life," he acknowledges the role of special religious practices, activities, and experiences. But he goes on to emphasize that to limit spirituality to these is to omit most of our life from spiritual living. To promote spiritual life, he says, is not to be more religious where one is already religious:

It is to be religious where he is irreligious now; to let the spiritual force which is in him play upon new activities. How shall he open, for instance, his business life to this deep power? By casting out of his business all that is essentially wicked in it, by insisting to himself on its ideal, of charity or usefulness, on the loftiest conception of every relationship into which it brings him with his fellow man, and by making it not a matter of his own whim or choice, but a duty to be done faithfully because God has called him to it. . . . God chose for him his work, and meant for him to find his spiritual education there.[1]

Brooks closed his sermon with these words: "The Christian finds the hand of Christ in everything, and by the faithful use of everything for Christ's sake, he takes firm hold of that hand of Christ and is drawn nearer and nearer to Himself. That is, I think, the best method of promoting spiritual life."

This steady stream of Christian spirituality through vocation flows down through the ages, and it alone is sufficient to the soul and to the world of humanity today. We have only to step into it, to set ourselves to learn it, and we will see its radiant power at work on the job where we are. If one will simply do what Bill Heatley says, he or she will find the promise, "I am with you always" (Matthew 28:20), to be the sure basis of abundance of life, whatever the job.

Dallas Willard

WORK — WHAT WAS GOD THINKING?

What is it to be a good person in business? . . . How to be a good person, that's where the light has gone out in our culture.
DALLAS WILLARD

I finished high school and ran right into work: BAM! One minute I was without a care in the world, and the next I was standing in the middle of a local amusement park sweeping up trash and being asked when the next show would begin. Beyond babysitting and mowing lawns, that was my first "real" job, and I've been working ever since. I found myself bouncing from job to job, seeking a few cents more an hour or simply moving on when the tedium and the people were too much to handle.

I worked hard and believed I would get ahead, and for the most part I was right. But there's a heavy price to success. A sacrifice must be made at the altar of getting ahead. My family paid the price for my hard work and success. After losing everything—my house, my cars, my marriage—and filing for bankruptcy, I finally woke up and realized that I didn't know the first thing about work. Indeed, I knew little about life. What I knew for sure was that work, as I understood it, couldn't be what God had in mind for me or for anyone else.

The more I looked for answers, the more confused I became. As my walk with Jesus deepened, it became more and more obvious that something was terribly wrong with my understanding about work. And I wasn't alone—I saw the problem everywhere. At work and in the daily newspaper, I saw a constant stream of Christians making questionable and unethical decisions and justifying or excusing every one. From Enron to the local banker and even in Christian organizations, everyone seemed lost and confused about work and what God intended. Greed, inhumanity, and survival of the fittest seemed to rule.

The power and destructive qualities of greed go underestimated. Look at Warner-Lambert's diabetes drug Rezulin and the sixty-plus deaths caused by the company's decision to intentionally hide adverse reactions to the drug and aggressively promote it to Hispanics because as a people group they trust their doctors and are more afraid of needles.[1]

Consider the self-induced travails of Enron, WorldCom, Arthur Anderson, Tyco International, Adelphia Communications, Rite Aid, Global Crossing, ImClone, KPMG, HomeStore, Citigroup, JPMorgan Chase, Merrill Lynch, Charles Schwab, Catholic Healthcare West, and Kaiser Permanente.[2] Exceptions? Exaggerations? Maybe. But not one of us is immune to the taint of questionable work. All of us are affected by the frequently self-centered beliefs that undergird the way we conduct business.

One way to think about this is to contrast a good person with a successful person. We think a good person is very different from a successful one. Review the responses I got from two high school English classes to two requests: "name someone successful" and "name someone good." For the first, they named a well-known billionaire, and for the second, an admired teacher. Then I asked them why the answers were different, why they defined success differently from goodness. As a clarifying point, since this was a Christian school, I asked them, "Was Jesus successful?"

The challenge for those students, and for all of us, is understanding that until we reconcile success with goodness, the world will tear us apart. The world will constantly pull us toward its definition of success and put us in tension with God's desire for goodness. *We will ruin our lives and hurt the people around us if we believe that goodness comes after we are successful.* That is serving two masters, God and money, and our lives will be confused and broken. Every day, work will ask us for more of our life, more of our time, and will lure us with a false version of success. We must find a place to stand firm in our knowledge of what is good and right in God's eyes.

FROM CURSE TO BLESSING

Jesus told His listeners, "Come to me, all you who are weary and burdened, and I will give you rest. Take my yoke upon you and learn from me, for I am gentle and humble in heart, and you will find rest for your souls. For my yoke is easy and my burden is light" (Matthew 11:28-30). And later, "And surely I am with you always, to the very end of the age" (Matthew 28:20).

For me, the false dichotomy between success and goodness began to reconcile when I really came to grips with the transforming reality of Jesus' kingdom undergirding my life and work. I will tell you how that realization occurred in the following chapter, but first I need to say that I came to understand, in a new way that I could enter into the astonishing reality of God's kingdom wherever I am, including at work. Jesus *is* with me to the end of the age, and that means I can look to Him to teach me, help me, and guide me in *all* that I do.

Hope is foundational for life, and today I have great hope about my work life. I am excited by the knowledge that the ember of God's love in His gift of work to humanity can be fanned into a flame of creative passion—as I express it daily in my work with others. With Him, in Him, and through Him our labors together become God's field, God's building, and an abundant blessing to those in need.

This book is about what I've learned about work in the kingdom of God. It concerns ideas that are crucial for making what we do for a living a place of discipleship. Along the way, I will share with you the insights I've learned, challenges I've faced, and practices that have helped strengthen me in my walk with Jesus. I'll also tell the stories of some Christians and companies that are laboring to make the good news of Jesus Christ manifest in this world of work.

SPIRITUAL DISCIPLINES FOR WORK

Some of the practices that have strengthened my kingdom perspective are called spiritual disciplines. I have found these to be crucial for my walk with God in and out of work, and I recommend them to you. Jesus considered spiritual disciplines integral to His life and ministry,[3] and as we read the Gospels we see Jesus taking opportunity to exercise these disciplines and ensure that His disciples were given the same opportunity and instruction. Spiritual disciplines aren't commandments, but Jesus holds them out to us as a master craftsman would to an apprentice. As Richard Foster put it in his book *Celebration of Discipline*, "God intends the Disciplines of the spiritual life to be for ordinary human beings: people who have jobs, who care for children, who must wash dishes and mow lawns."[4]

Douglas Rumford said, "In themselves spiritual disciplines can do nothing; they can only get us to a place where something can be done."[5] That posture of dependence on God is uncomfortable for most people today. The word *discipline* also has a somewhat negative connotation in our quick-fix society, so it might be helpful to think about them in terms of "spiritual training," "holy habits," "spiritual fitness," or something similar.

I AM NOT ALONE

I can see now that God had a plan for me to learn the nature and purpose of work as He intends it. He had a plan for me to realize the great blessing and benefit of work to me and everyone around me. He provided me with someone to help me on my journey of discovering the joy of work in His kingdom. He brought someone into my life to guide me, mentor me, and be my spiritual friend: Dallas Willard. Dallas has helped me see what God intended when He created work, and he shows me by his living example how to do my job. Dallas, who asks that I refer to him simply as "a fellow pilgrim," has opened up the history and writings of holy men who have come before us in discovering the great wonder and beauty of work. Much of what I know about work and many of the writings of those that have come before I owe to his guidance. Dallas's wisdom and experience with God's living Word has brought the Bible to a fuller and richer level in my heart. His love of God and the gentleness that it brings to everyone and everything around him, is an example for me and others.

John Ortberg, someone else who has been influenced by Dallas, says,

> The circle of people who have been influenced by his life is a very wide one, and to spend much time with him at all is to recognize that this is a person who has entered a long ways into a life most of us only loiter at the edges of. More than his writings and thought, helpful as those are, it is his simplicity and humility and ability to attend to the moment and to whomever he is with that bring hope that such a life as Jesus promises really is possible.[6]

With an abundance of God's grace, Dallas has helped steady my steps and unveiled God's truth about work. My confusion has continued to clear, and seeing what God intended for my job has transformed it into one of the great joys and blessings in my life. Deep wisdom about work is something that everyone in the workplace should have. That's why I wrote this book. My prayer is that it will help you answer the question, "Work — what was God thinking?" and grant you the wisdom and peace the answer has brought me. It's a wisdom that inspired A. P. Giannini, the founder of Bank of America, to say, "Serving the needs of others is the only legitimate business in the world today."

CHAPTER ONE

CHANGING OUR MINDS ABOUT WORK

"It is the Lord Christ whom you serve." This is a radical change in the understanding of what work is, what a job is, what business is, and it can only be understood in the context of the kingdom of God. I'm not going to try to exhort you to get God into business, I'm just going to explain to you two main ways that He is in business, and we have to come to terms with it, because He is there.

DALLAS WILLARD

In 1974, Studs Terkel wrote,

Work, by its very nature, [is] about violence—to the spirit as well as to the body. It is about ulcers as well as accidents, about shouting matches as well as fist-fights, about nervous breakdowns as well as kicking the dog around. It is, above all (or beneath all), about daily humiliations. To survive the day is triumph enough for the walking wounded among the great many of us.[1]

This was my experience with work for many years, and I know so many people who live with work as a "daily humiliation."

In my deepest despair about work, God threw me a lifeline. Frustrated and struggling, I was convinced work was all about money, power, and domination. Whatever God might have originally intended, human greed had taken over. Work was a curse. Work was a place of toil, anguish, and mind-numbing labor for someone else's benefit. The best you could hope for was to survive the day, eke out a living, and look ahead to something better in the future. So I was shocked when I asked a fellow pilgrim for his thoughts and he answered, "Work, and on a broader scale, business, is a fundamental structure of love in the kingdom of God." He went on to tell me that God's purpose for work is to "bring people together in loving community for mutual benefit and support."

I was stunned. Absolutely stunned. In one sweep of God's mighty hand, all my ideas about work had been shattered and miraculously rebuilt into something beautiful and beyond my imagining. At that moment, I felt like I had just stepped on a live wire. The powerful cleansing truth of what this fellow pilgrim said left me forever changed. The effect wasn't limited to my ideas about work but penetrated deeply into how I thought and felt about God. That God created work as a place of love—a place where I could be nurtured and supported, a place where I could contribute and flourish—continues to amaze and delight me.

Sure, my old thoughts still lingered on. My old habits born of the "daily humiliations" and my own greed and confusion continued to affect me. But from that point on, nothing about work or my life has ever been the same. Years of struggle and fruitless attempts to reconcile my work with my discipleship to Jesus Christ were somehow deeply resolved.

The years since that conversation have been remarkable, and what I've learned is that work *is* a fundamental structure of love in the kingdom of God. God *meant* for us to come together in loving community so we could benefit from and support each other. Work stands beside all the other loving structures He created for us—marriage, friendship, family, and nature. God intends work to be the firm support beneath, around, and within a community, so that *all* the people in that community—regardless of their age, sex, color, belief, or ability—can use their unique gifts and skills to provide for one another's needs. No one is excluded, everyone is welcome, and everyone is needed to contribute and be blessed in return. God wants us to reign in the marvelous kingdom that He gives us (our life), to be fruitful, loving, and caring with the "garden" He has given us so that others are blessed.

When we bring our job into the kingdom of God, by aligning it with His divine purpose for work and inviting Him in, our efforts unite with His in miraculous and supernatural ways. Our job is nourished, sustained, and empowered by the mighty arm of God. I want Him in my life so I begin each day with God and show my gratitude to Him each week in my tithes and offerings. I call these practices "first fruits."

FIRST FRUITS

My idols were time and money—I could never get enough of either one. I would do almost anything to get more of them so I could spend them as I wished, and that desire pushed God out of my life. Somewhere along the way, I realized who God was and who I was—and I stopped. First fruits—the giving of the first part of my day and the first check that I write after payday—have replaced my selfish pursuits. This principle comes from the Old Testament practice of offering your first fruits of the harvest to God. Time and money are the things that I "harvest." So I tithe my income, and I offer the first fruits of each day. I get up thirty minutes earlier than I used to and give that time to God. Every day starts with God—in prayer and study of and meditation on His Word. It is the single most important thing I do, and it starts the day better than anything I know.

Rather than taking time away from my too-busy schedule, this practice magnifies my time and provides me with more time to do the things I should be doing. On several occasions, I've had to choose between an early-morning meeting and my time with God. Every time I chose God, He's cleared the way by lightening the traffic flow, or perhaps canceling or rescheduling the meeting. The money is also something I don't miss, and I am far richer for having given it to Him.

I've spoken with several Christian CEOs who set aside the first part of their day to be with God, and they all confirm how richly they are blessed throughout the day as a result. I've also found many companies that have early morning Bible studies and a growing number of commuters who use their early morning commute to listen to the Bible or inspirational books or Christian radio. These practices prepare you for the day by bringing God in before you start. (Throughout this book I will be giving examples of spiritual disciplines tailored expressly for the workplace. Each is described with a brief explanation of how you can practice it.)

> **PRACTICE·** The obsessive pursuit of time and money is the primary issue for Christians in the workplace today. Finding ways to let go and give those things back to God is essential in our walk with Him. Begin with five or ten minutes each morning in prayer and reading the Bible. Steadily increase until the first thirty minutes of your day is spent with God. The day that you get paid, write a check to God for the amount you have agreed to give. Steadily increase to 10 percent.

Starting our day with God makes it easier to bring Him with us into our work. With Him on our mind and in our heart as we begin our job, we increasingly become aware that He is with us and more easily bring Him into what we are doing. We are renewed and refreshed by interacting with God in our daily routine. Our work is transformed from something the world has ruined into an activity and a place of love and Immanuel (God with us) potential. It is transformed from "daily humiliations" into an abundant garden overflowing with "love, joy, peace, patience, kindness, goodness, faithfulness, gentleness and self-control" (see the "fruit of the Spirit" in Galatians 5:22-23).

THE CREATION OF WORK

In Genesis 2:15, we read, "The LORD God took the man and put him in the Garden of Eden to work it and take care of it." From the beginning, work and care[2] have been bonded together under God. The loving nature of work can be seen in its unblemished beginning. In their tending of the garden, Adam and Eve would find purpose and fulfillment. Their work and care would result in a thriving, beautiful garden that would satisfy their needs. God would be present in the garden with them, His loving hand upon them and their lives. Caring is central—God never intended work to be estranged from caring or to occur outside His kingdom. Work shouldn't be separated from caring any more than loving God should be separated from loving our neighbor. For work to be the blessing God intended, we must give it back to Him—to work in love "as to the Lord" (Colossians 3:23, KJV) and to care for those with whom we work.

For the most part, our society excludes caring and God from work. This helps explain why work can be so numbing, draining, and dehumanizing—and how it got to be "about violence" and "daily humiliations." Without caring or God, work becomes a place of violence, greed, and destruction. Without *caring* as the underlying attitude, the garden God has provided to each one of us will continue to wither and die. Examples of this in today's world are pollution as a result of unrivaled technical advance, untreated but curable diseases (for example, malaria), moral corruption of well-educated leaders, and death from starvation while food is hoarded in lands of plenty.

Work becomes a thing to be squeezed, something to be used up and discarded as we move on to greener pastures. When our work involves service, without *caring* as a fundamental part of how the work is performed, it is people (employees, customers, and society) who are used up and discarded. If work involves creating useful products, then it is resources (air, water, minerals, food, land, animals) that are used up and discarded along with the people. No lasting good is achieved—the value is squeezed out and the empty husk thrown away. We don't have to look very far to see the wake of destruction that uncaring businesses have left behind: lives ruined, communities decimated and impoverished, natural resources and wilderness polluted.

Think about your job. Do you feel like you're working in a beautiful garden where your needs are met in a loving community? When you consider your work, do the words *love, care, joy, garden, lasting good, mutual benefit,* and *support* come to mind? For many, work elicits other terms, many that shouldn't be printed. But that's where God comes in.

MY OWN EXPERIENCE

As information technology director of a large insurance company, I managed a department of twelve people who were responsible for the computer systems that supported the company's human resource and payroll departments along with several other areas. My staff worked with HR and payroll to make sure that employees were compensated accurately (rate, vacation time, deductions, taxes) and on time. For multiple reasons, this job required people to regularly work twelve- to sixteen-hour days, often until 2:00 or 3:00 a.m., whenever payroll was run. It was a hard and thankless job.

Two things struck me about my staff: their total dedication to the job and their hatred of it. They all wanted out. My staff didn't see any value in what they were doing, and the future didn't look any brighter. As far as they were concerned, quitting seemed to be their only hope. It was a challenging situation. The human resource department thought very little of them (so much for the *human* part of their title). The employees that benefited from their dedication and hard work didn't know or care that they existed—they just wanted their paycheck. My department was understaffed, underpaid, and had been given little or no training. All of these conditions contributed to their disdain for the work, and previous management had done nothing to address any of these issues.

I decided to stand in the gap and give God space to work in my job. I decided to take intentional steps in trying to create and grow a godly environment of loving community and mutual benefit and support. In the first staff meeting I held with my team, I went over a few simple things: I thanked them for making sure that everyone in the company was paid on time without fail, and I told them that the work they did had value. I explained the benefit they brought to each and every employee. I told them that I believed in them: I believed that they were there to do a good job and that I could trust them to do their best. I asked them about areas of greatest difficulty and suggestions for making improvements. Over the next few months, I worked hard to address their needs and concerns.

I requested additional staff and funding for training, and I received both. I worked on building mutual respect and understanding between my department and the HR and payroll departments. It took time to build trust, but we did. The individuals in my department went from being cliquish and antagonistic to working well together as a team and sharing more of themselves and caring more for each other. The department went for sixteen months with zero turnover (an unheard-of statistic in that company since the average was 30 percent turnover in twelve months). There are so many more examples of what God was doing on a day-to-day basis that it would fill another book. I've learned what happens when you let God in at work, and nothing compares to the wonder and power of seeing His hand working with you and through you. I can say with confidence, "Be strong and courageous. Do not be terrified; do not be discouraged, for the LORD your God will be with you wherever you go" (Joshua 1:9). Surely, one place the Lord our God will go is with us into our workplace—if only we will invite Him to walk beside us.

WORKING WITH GOD

I often wonder what it was like in the original garden before humans lost confidence in God. Think about it—an unblemished landscape, fruitful labor, abundant harvest, harmony between God and all of His creation, reigned over by Adam and Eve working hand in hand with God. Everything around them was created, upheld, and sustained by the spoken word of God. I wonder: Was the power of God manifest in their tending of the garden? Does Matthew 21:21 give us a hint of what it must have been like? "I tell you the truth, if you have faith and do not doubt . . . you can say to this mountain, 'Go, throw yourself into the sea,' and it will be done." Moving mountains, tilling the ground, naming the animals—what do you think they did together? What would *you* do in their situation? I've often imagined how I would arrange the garden, where I would put the mountains, how I would make the streams run so they would catch the sunlight, and how I would have an orchard of all my favorite fruit trees. In my own backyard, I'm going to plant three fruit trees; I've got to dig up old stumps and ivy, prepare the soil, buy the trees, drive them home, and plant them. But in that first garden, Adam probably could've said, "Let's put an avocado on the left and an orange tree on the right," and it was done. Ah, those were the days.

We are created in God's image, and part of that image includes the desire and ability to create. Adam and Eve's work in the garden was one outlet for their creativity. Our work is to be an outlet for our creative goodness as well. I believe God wants us to envision and live a life of goodness and beauty where we care for creation side by side with God. He calls us to a life where our work creates a garden of grace, peace, provision, and love for all those who enter in. Just as God helped Adam and Eve with the heavy lifting in the garden, He will help us to renew and transform the garden that He has given to us. No matter how barren or desolate our garden might seem, with God, what can't be accomplished?

Remember Israel during the time of the Exile, when Jerusalem had been reduced to burned rubble and Nehemiah and Ezra returned to rebuild the wall and the Temple? It's a great story of God's people coming together to restore what sin had destroyed. Maybe a clear vision of life in the garden can inspire us to reclaim and begin rebuilding what was damaged in the Fall.

PRACTICE MAKING SPACE FOR GOD

In order for us to work with God, we first have to make a space for Him and then invite Him in. Our experience of God's presence in our workplace has to do with how much we let Him in, how much space we make for Him in our job. Jesus knew this was a matter of heart, and He used the image of a good tree bearing good fruit to symbolize a heart that is open to God and bearing the fruit of a good life (see Matthew 7:18). How can we perform our job so that God has a space to work with us, through us, and around us? How can we increasingly participate in the amazing community of redeemed souls that God dwells in for eternity? You make a space for God when you do something you can't do without Him. You take a risk (with the potential of failure on human terms) and then rest in the power and provision of God (the kingdom of the heavens) because you trust (have faith in) Jesus and enjoy growing in knowledge (experiencing God).

The apostle Paul points us toward the answers when he writes, "What, after all, is Apollos? And what is Paul? Only servants, through whom you came to believe—as the Lord has assigned to each his task. I planted the seed, Apollos watered it, but God made it grow" (1 Corinthians 3:5-6). We do our job in a way that lets God in. We cooperate with others in a spirit of humility, service, and mutual support. We give God's Spirit the freedom to enhance and enrich our work.

We make a space for God by loving those around us through intentional acts of support, celebration, and appreciation. We pray for the success of others' good works. We intentionally celebrate the value and contributions of those around us and openly express our appreciation for them. We do a good job regardless of who's watching and praising us. Combined, these practices form a discipline that opens a space around us for God's love, creates a space for God to be made manifest, and helps unseat pride from our heart. It is a discipline that embodies the verse, "Do nothing out of selfish ambition or vain conceit, but in humility consider others better than yourselves" (Philippians 2:3). This practice helps us see people from God's perspective—those unique and beautiful aspects of who they are regardless of their position and authority. It helps us view their work in the context of God's kingdom as they provide a vital benefit to others. This discipline helps us be mindful of how these men and women contribute to God's loving plan to provide for His people, and how I can help them accomplish it.

A dramatic experience of this discipline came when I had just started a new job. I was working with someone from another department to prepare for a very important meeting. She was diligent, thorough, upbeat, and her attention to detail set the stage for a smooth meeting. However, the department that I worked for had a lot of history with her department, and it was like the Hatfields and McCoys—simmering tension and periodic hostilities. So I did three simple things: I prayed for her, I thanked her management in another meeting, and I sent an e-mail to her boss expressing my appreciation for her hard work (I made a space for God to fill). The effect was immediate and beyond any reasonable explanation by my efforts. Eighteen months of growing tensions eased, and a period of greater cooperation ensued. Was there perfect harmony? No. Was there still friction and minor feuding? Yes. But the thorny issues became far less important than the enjoyment of working together. We learned how to work toward a common goal and found mutual support along the way (I planted, she watered, God made it grow). I found a way to do my task and make a space for God to fill, and in the process my faith and knowledge of God increased. And just as Solomon prayed when the presence of the Lord filled the temple, I could pray,

> O LORD, God of Israel, there is no God like you in heaven above or on earth below—you who keep your covenant of love with your servants who continue wholeheartedly in your way. . . . With your mouth you have promised and with your hand you have fulfilled it—as it is today. (1 Kings 8:23-24)

PRACTICE· Pray for the success of those around you. In a public setting, sincerely compliment someone who deserves it. Go out of your way to help someone even if it isn't your job.

WATCHING AND WAITING

This discipline is a natural part of all other disciplines and is extremely beneficial when partnered with prayer and making a space for God. "Watching and waiting" means patiently and expectantly looking for what God is doing—for how His character and power are manifest. We tend to seek a specific and immediate outcome from our efforts. We work toward a goal and get frustrated at ourselves and others when it doesn't happen *immediately!* Watching and waiting teaches us to let God be God. His time is not our time. Watching and waiting teaches us to put God in charge of outcomes and keeps our focus on doing what's right and doing our best.

If prayer is being caught up in what you and God are doing together, then watching and waiting is the other half of that friendship. It can be a discipline on its own, and through it you will improve your vision of "him who is invisible" (Hebrews 11:27). Watching and waiting will focus your mind on God and push against your natural tendency toward hurry and distraction. Jesus told His disciples to "watch and pray" (Matthew 26:41). Had they followed His instruction, they would not have succumbed to the weakness of their flesh and fallen asleep. Paul tells us to "walk circumspectly" (Ephesians 5:15, KJV)—to look around and pay attention. In Micah 7:7 we read, "But as for me, I watch in hope for the LORD, I wait for God my Savior; my God will hear me."

Examples of where to practice this discipline are meetings where you are seeking a specific decision from executives, team projects, and employee reviews (yours and other people's). Every task we do has an outcome that rightly belongs to God. My yearly review is a great example of practicing this discipline. In years past, I would make sure that my boss was keenly aware of how great I was doing. I would even go so far as to delay bad news around review time. That did three things: (1) It focused my attention away from my job, (2) elevated dishonesty instead of truth, and (3) led me to trust myself and not God. I was managing outcomes (my career, my boss's opinion of me, and my salary). Now it is far more important to me that God be honored than it is to be falsely advanced.

When you first practice this discipline, things can be a little confusing. Where do you draw the line? How do you know when to turn it over to God, and what is enough? Wisdom and discernment will come, I've found, if we rely on God's Word, advice from trusted spiritual advisors, and this hard and fast rule: *No future good justifies a present evil.* As the proverb says, "When the storm has swept by, the wicked are gone, but the righteous stand firm forever" (10:25).

> **PRACTICE·** Pray for a specific person at work consistently for two weeks and watch for God's presence. Make a space for God in your daily tasks and watch and pray. Patiently keep your eyes, ears, and heart open to what God does.

WORK IN GOD'S CONTEXT

Work can seem very far removed from God and the caring He intended, but at its heart, work remains one of the principal means that God created to provide for His people. When we leave home and head for work, it should be with the encouragement that the next portion of our day is going to be spent helping to meet the needs of people in the community our business serves.

Work as a structure of love consists of three elements: provision, goodness, and security.

Provision is the "supplies" or resources that will meet needs — food, clothing, housing, justice, medical care, art, or information — and these supplies come from the abundance that God has provided in and around us. The apostle Paul speaks to this concept:

> Now he who supplies seed to the sower and bread for food will also supply and increase your store of seed and will enlarge the harvest of your righteousness. You will be made rich in every way so that you can be generous on every occasion, and through us your generosity will result in thanksgiving to God. (2 Corinthians 9:10-11)

Goodness is having a heart to love others and wanting to provide for them what is good and best. It is not by chance that the word *goods* uses the same root as *goodness* and that both trace their core meaning back to God.

Security is protecting and promoting what is good and eliminating or suppressing what is evil. Securing the lives of the people in a community by ensuring that the sources of provision and goodness are maintained allows a just and merciful society to flourish and bless. Isaiah 32:2 embraces all three elements of the work structure:

> Each man will be like a shelter from the wind
> and a refuge from the storm,

like streams of water in the desert
  and the shadow of a great rock in a thirsty land.

With this understanding about work as a fundamental structure of love, we can engage verses like 1 Corinthians 15:58 in a new way. We can see a new life in God's kingdom that includes our job: "Therefore, my dear brothers, stand firm. Let nothing move you. Always give yourselves fully to the work of the Lord, because you know that your labor in the Lord is not in vain." Seeing God within the fundamental structure of work through His abundant providence, loving goodness, and everlasting security helps us walk with Him and invite His full participation in our vocation.

Getting ready for my workday is markedly different for me since I came to understand work as God intended. I used to plot, plan, and worry about how I was going to deal with all my problems and adversaries. How was I going to get ahead today? I was tense and ready to rumble before I got out of my car. Now I bring the wisdom of Peter's words with me to work:

Above all, love each other deeply, because love covers over a multitude of sins. Offer hospitality to one another without grumbling. Each one should use whatever gift he has received to serve others, faithfully administering God's grace in its various forms. If anyone speaks, he should do it as one speaking the very words of God. If anyone serves, he should do it with the strength God provides, so that in all things God may be praised through Jesus Christ. To him be the glory and the power for ever and ever. Amen. (1 Peter 4:8-11)

I submit my body and my job to God and ask Him for help. I seek to know and be in His will and find His provision, goodness, and security throughout my day.

MUTUAL BENEFIT AND SUPPORT

Work is about people. Not indirectly, but directly and in all aspects. It is performed with people, done by people and for people. There is no work, as we understand it, without people. So the purpose of work rightly begins by bringing people together, and in that way work is an extension of the loving family structure. It also means that work is for everyone, and everyone who can contribute and provide value, should. No one should be excluded. I spotted an excellent example of this in an article featuring Habitat International, Inc.:

> Explaining why his company was so successful, CEO David Morris said: "I hire the people no one else wants to hire." Schizophrenics drive forklifts next to those with Down syndrome, autism, and cerebral palsy. Recovering alcoholics, deaf employees, and homeless people cut floor runners alongside co-workers who have suffered strokes, severe head injuries, or loss of an arm. All are cross-trained on every task in the plant. "We have practically no absenteeism and very little turnover. We've also seen higher production, increased profits, better morale, greater respect from the community, and better customer relationships."[3]

Once people have been brought together, loving community is the best way of working. We understand and appreciate love covering over a multitude of sins. I know I'm not perfect, and in my efforts I sometimes offend and cause hurt. Love becomes the means of bridging the gaps and healing the wounds that I cause. The tensions that our unique differences and limitations might cause are transformed into dynamic and diverse strengths through love.

In his book *The Fabric of This World*, Lee Hardy states, "We all have needs which we alone cannot meet. By necessity we live in communities of interdependent individuals. And we are to make use of what talents we do have to serve others as they, in turn, serve us." He also shares a summary of John Calvin's teaching on the book of Galatians, saying: "He [God] intended us to live in a community of mutual love and service."[4]

It's a simple concept that is sorely missing from our world. Part of being a Christian is finding ways to illuminate what is good. Point it out, talk about it, promote it wherever we find it. Doing our job to the very best of our unique abilities supports others and opens our work to receive the benefit of our labors.

Imagine a workplace with people who embrace this philosophy of work as God intended. People will learn to understand, appreciate, and cherish the unique qualities and contributions of others. In turn they will be understood, appreciated, and cherished for their own unique contributions. Differences and conflict will be resolved in love, without intentionally hurting someone, engaging in politics, or ignoring the problem. The vocabulary and attitudes about work will change. Words like *love*, *trust*, *care*, *understanding*, and *joy* will begin to appear in normal conversation about work.

Think about Paul's description of the body in 1 Corinthians 12 as a business analogy for loving community. It's an excellent illustration of how our talents and natural giftedness can benefit a community by placing each of us in dependence upon one another. The body cannot properly function without all its needed parts. Work is advanced when each of us contributes our special giftedness and appreciates the contribution of others.

THE DISCIPLINE OF RELATIONSHIP

When you work with people, it's important to invite God into those relationships. It's wise to bring Him in and to ask Him to wrap His arms around all of you. Relationship discipline calls us to remember our relationship with Jesus, who He is, what He has done for us, and what He calls us to. Jesus presents this God-based relationship in His analogy of a vine:

> I am the true vine, and my Father is the gardener. He cuts off every branch in me that bears no fruit, while every branch that does bear fruit he prunes so that it will be even more fruitful. You are already clean because of the word I have spoken to you. Remain in me, and I will remain in you. No branch can bear fruit by itself; it must remain in the vine. Neither can you bear fruit unless you remain in me.
>
> I am the vine; you are the branches. If a man remains in me and I in him, he will bear much fruit; apart from me you can do nothing. If anyone does not remain in me, he is like a branch that is thrown away and withers; such branches are picked up, thrown into the fire and burned. If you remain in me and my words remain in you, ask whatever you wish, and it will be given you. This is to my Father's glory, that you bear much fruit, showing yourselves to be my disciples. (John 15:1-8)

Jesus asks us to extend to others what we have been freely given — Himself. You hold the key to letting Jesus into the midst of your relationships. Remember to open the door for Jesus in all of your relationships: enemy, friend, coworker, neighbor, stranger. Relationship calls us to serve and support others as in Ephesians 4:28-29:

> He who has been stealing must steal no longer, but must work, doing something useful with his own hands, that he may have something to share with those in need. Do not let any unwholesome talk come out of your mouths, but only what is helpful for building others up according to their needs, that it may benefit those who listen.

Stealing breaks relationship; it is the antithesis of loving community and mutual benefit and support. Stealing can be something as benign as delegating our work to others or letting someone else carry a heavier workload. Our actions should contribute to the needs of others, and our words must build others up and benefit those who listen.

Relationship is being a servant to others. Jesus tells us in Mark 10:43-45: "Whoever wants to become great among you must be your servant, and whoever wants to be first must be slave of all. For even the Son of Man did not come to be served, but to serve, and to give his life as a ransom for many." If God came as a servant, who are we to put ourselves above others? How can I apply this teaching to my job? How should I be a "servant" and "slave of all"? By embracing what God intended, His will, about work. Loving community relies upon loving relationships, and loving relationships must first remember Jesus, who He is, what He has done for us, and what He calls us to. Second, we must follow Him by loving others—build others up, be a servant, and don't steal. In this way, we ensure that even at work His will is being done on earth as it is in heaven.

PRACTICE· Evaluate your job and make sure you are bearing the full weight of your responsibilities. Take time to give an accounting to God for your actions. Don't steal. Remember Jesus and find ways to bring Him into all your relationships. Generously build others up. Be a servant to others—find and promote what is good at work, stand firm, be a refuge to others in a storm. Do all that you can to create, promote, and enhance a loving community at work. Ensure that all your dealings with others achieve mutual benefit and support, first for them and then for you. And above all else, seek God at all times and in all things. See others as God sees them, not as you wish them to be.

CHAPTER TWO

KINGDOM LIVING

I especially like 2 Chronicles 16:9: The eyes of the Lord run to and fro throughout the whole earth, to show Himself strong, on behalf of those whose hearts are fixed upon Him. *That's a basic picture that we must never forget. God is on the job, business is His business, humanity is not a human project, humanity is God's project, and He is bringing out of it an amazing community of redeemed souls, which He will dwell in for eternity. And we each get to be a part of that.*

DALLAS WILLARD

The gospel Jesus preached was the kingdom of God (the kingdom of the heavens). He talked about it, He lived it, and He provides us with an array of comparisons and parables about His Father's kingdom. So what is it? The kingdom of God is a kingdom of power. It is God in action (see 1 Corinthians 4:20). The kingdom of God is the range of God's effective will or where His will is done.[1] When we say, "Thy will be done on earth as it is in heaven," we are asking for God's will to be done in our kingdom the same way that God's will is done in heaven (perfectly).

So God gives each one of us a kingdom. What makes up our

kingdom? Our kingdom is our life, the range of our effective will or what we have say over. It's challenging to think we have a kingdom in today's world, but we do. Jesus gives a complete and accurate description of our kingdom in Mark 12:29-31; it is comprised of our heart, soul, mind, strength, and our relationships. Together they make up our life. Obedience to God, doing His will, and being a disciple of Christ mean putting God on the throne of our kingdom and seeking to have our life be what God wants it to be. It also means trusting Him with our life and letting His love permeate every aspect of our life, His kingdom come.

KINGDOM RULE

I emphasize kingdom to better appreciate the direct application of bib-lical teaching about kings. The Bible is full of stories about kings and kingdoms, but we are apt to hold them at a distance if we don't think we have a kingdom of our own. They had a job, we have a job — just because their title was king doesn't exclude their experiences from helping us.

There were good kings, evil kings, and mediocre kings (for exam-ple, respectively, Josiah, Ahab, and Jehoshaphat). The good kings ruled their kingdom with a heart for God, like David and Josiah: "David reigned over all Israel, doing what was just and right for all his people" (2 Samuel 8:15). At a young age, when David was a shepherd protecting his flock, he fought and killed lions and bears, and he learned that it was done with the strength of the Lord. This knowledge and experience of God's power gave David confidence in God, and those early lessons taught him how to walk in the character and power of God. With confidence grounded in personal experience, David could tell Goliath, "I come against you in the name of the LORD Almighty" (1 Samuel 17:45). David learned how to walk and talk with God in every job he had — shepherd, soldier, prophet, poet, king.

Josiah inherited his job. He truly loved God and was anguished when he discovered how distant his kingdom was from God. He dedicated the rest of his life to being obedient to God and determined "to follow the LORD and keep his commands, regulations and decrees with all his heart and all his soul" (2 Kings 23:3). Josiah experienced the awesome power of God's hand throughout the rest of His reign, and God blessed him. Both of these kings sought God in all they did and let Him guide and strengthen them through good times and bad. They weren't perfect, but their love for God was the center of their lives.

YOU GOTTA HAVE HEART

David and Josiah experienced the supernatural hand of God. They lived their lives and did their jobs in such a way that God was made manifest. As disciples of Christ Jesus, we must also expect that when we open our lives to Him, He will be present. We must adopt a way of life that helps us grow in our knowledge of God so we can stand and be steady in the face of our own Goliath. We might not be kings, but we have a kingdom, and God has work for us to accomplish with Him in the kingdom He has given. So how do we do our jobs in a way that honors God? How do we live our lives in such a way that we experience the supernatural hand of God in what we are doing? One way is by learning from Jesus how to live, by studying His life. We can identify the things He did when He wasn't being pressured by the crowds and Pharisees and apply them to our own life. These disciplines will help us stand and be steady in the face of all that the world throws at us (see Ephesians 6:13).

As followers of Jesus, we read, study, and meditate on what He said and did; we look closely at how He lived His life. He wants us to trust Him, to be His students and friends. He promises to make our burdens light and easy if we will learn from Him, bind ourselves to Him, and allow Him to show us the way (see Matthew 11:28-30). So this is where we should begin: following the way of living that Jesus provides to us. His life had a pattern of obedience, submission, and the regular practice of the spiritual disciplines. When you read the Gospels, you gain a clear sense that Jesus sought time for solitude and prayer with His Father. He regularly practiced and taught to His disciples the spiritual disciplines that He knew were important: fasting from food and sleep (sometimes referred to as the discipline of watching), solitude, frugality, sacrificial giving, and prayer. He took very intentional steps to draw near to His Father even in the face of great demands.[2]

There are two reasons to practice the spiritual disciplines: first, the benefit and blessing of a disciplined life, and second, the example and teachings of Jesus. The first we wisely accept as we look at any field of endeavor. No one can achieve success without practice — pianists, baseball players, painters, or surgeons. Every pursuit is benefited by practice, training, and refinement of technique. This wisdom extends to our character and behavior and also extends to our spiritual formation.

The second reason is why I personally feel a need to practice the spiritual disciplines: I practice them because Jesus practiced them. He believed they were important enough to teach to His followers. In turn, they knew the disciplines were important enough that they taught them to new followers. And I am not beyond needing their blessing or following their advice. Spiritual disciplines are a means of allowing God access to my heart so He can change and transform me. As Jesus tells us, "The good man brings good things out of the good stored up in his heart. . . . For out of the overflow of his heart his mouth speaks" (Luke 6:45).

Heart, spirit, and will all refer to the same seat of our thoughts and actions. They all represent the center of our life. From that center we choose to act or not, to speak or remain silent. When we ask God to transform us, we are asking to be remade into the likeness of Christ, asking for our heart to be like His.

KNEE-JERK REACTION

We all agree that we should turn the other cheek, bless those who curse us, and love our enemies. But on our own, can we? Many of us have trouble getting out of the church parking lot without a disparaging thought, word, or gesture. The extreme but all-too-frequent forms of these reactions have nicknames: "Going postal," "They pushed my buttons," "I just lost it," "I snapped," "I lost my head," "I lost my cool," and "I bit off her head." These expressions and many others like them indicate our "natural" tendency toward hurtful, thoughtless reaction.

Paul understood this situation and in Romans 7:23 says, "I see another law at work in the members of my body, waging war against the law of my mind and making me a prisoner of the law of sin at work within my members." The "law of sin at *work* within my members" indicates that our bodies are predisposed and conditioned to react in certain ways, that sin literally inhabits our arm, tongue, or whatever body part is involved, and that in the heat of the moment the sinful reaction of the member involved is virtually guaranteed. As much as we would like to discount and discredit these events as not being who we "really are," they expose a part of us that truly needs God. How we react is sometimes a more healthy and truthful gauge in determining how far we have come in becoming more Christlike. C. S. Lewis provides a pointed insight in his book *Mere Christianity*:

> Surely what a man does when he is taken off his guard is the best evidence for what sort of a man he is? Surely what pops out before the man has time to put on a disguise is the truth? If there are rats in a cellar, you are most likely to see them if you go in very suddenly. But the suddenness does not create the rats: it only prevents them from hiding.[3]

Most of us would like to completely ignore these moments and not count them in any analysis or evaluation of our "true intentions." We believe these moments, along with all the other times where we were under too much stress or when we had a lapse of judgment for some reason or other, should be excluded from any fair analysis. We beg and plead to have them excluded, but they must be included and given the greatest weight if we are to truly know ourselves on the inside. They are, as C. S. Lewis tells us, "the best evidence for what sort of man" we are.

HELPFUL HABITS

Think of habits as "consistent reactions." They might be good or evil, but God has blessed us with the ability to form habits. Driving is, hopefully, a good example of how we physically train ourselves to react the way we intend without having to think before we act. When you were learning to drive, you consciously had to tell yourself to brake, turn, check your mirrors, accelerate, and signal. We recognize the danger of having to think in a driving emergency, and we rely on our trained responses and reflexes to guide us safely through those situations. We understand that only repetition and practice can fulfill this need. Training in sports and music provide similar examples of good habits being formed.

All behavior training—twelve-step programs, Weight Watchers, boot camp—focuses on identifying and breaking old bad habits and forming new good ones. But forming new habits, however good they might be, can never be a complete answer, because life can be very different from the conditions we trained in. Habits are crucial and beneficial, but if they are all we have, then the dynamics of life will cause them to be insufficient in certain unpredictable situations. More frequently than we care to realize, it is our heart that determines our action.

That is why Jesus focused on the heart and taught us that it's our heart that needs to be good. Then, no matter what the situation, good fruit will be born. We still need habits and can wisely form them to help us lead godly lives, but we should also take appropriate action to allow God to transform our hearts. That is where Jesus' example of spiritual disciplines is so valuable. He shows us how to change our hearts and submit our bodies to God (which will drive sin from our members).[4] We must let God in and let Him transform our whole life—heart, mind, soul, strength, and relationships. In his book *Renovation of the Heart*, Dallas Willard says:

> Spiritual formation in Christ obviously requires that we increasingly be happily reconciled to living in and by *the direct upholding of the hand of God*. This is clearly what the entire biblical view of life calls for, and especially what Jesus himself lived and presented as the truth. Only from within this gospel outlook on life can we begin to approach the godly reformation of the self in its social world. But from within that outlook we can cease from assault and withdrawal and can extend ourselves in blessing to all whose lives we touch.[5]

In my own experience, when I follow Jesus' example, I am transformed through God's grace. The things that I struggled with on my own—lying, fear of confrontation, failure to follow-through, procrastination—He is able to address. The spiritual disciplines bring me to a place where I can delight in the Lord and receive the desire of my heart (Psalm 37:4). Until that happens I am content with each "thorn" (thorns are not necessarily sins). The regular practice of spiritual disciplines opens my life to God's transforming power unlike anything I know and I wholeheartedly recommend them to you.

LIAR, LIAR, PANTS ON FIRE

I used to lie at work. I lied as easily as I breathed, especially when it involved bad news about something for which I was responsible. I would say what I thought people wanted to hear or what I wanted them to think and then go try to make it true. People admired my ability to make things happen, which I did well, but they learned to question what I said. I didn't want to live that way. I couldn't stand telling a lie—it made me feel weak, and it bothered me that I didn't trust God enough to tell the truth.

I recall a time when my team and I were going to miss a deadline for a critical project. I knew it, the team knew it, and it was time to report the problem. Instead, I lied. I reported that the project would be finished on time. And then I went to the team and yelled and bullied and tried every trick I knew to meet the deadline. It made no difference—in fact, it just made matters worse. Now I had two problems: missing the deadline and being identified as unreliable (business speak for a liar). I hated every moment.

I set out to have God change that part of me, and over the course of two years I worked on my lying. It became a consistent focus in my prayers, devotions, and times of solitude and fasting. When I failed, I would ask God for forgiveness and press on. I remember one specific occasion when I realized that He had changed my heart. I had bad news to report about a project. Though tempted to lie or deflect as I'd done in the past, I prayed, I told the truth . . . and I lived. I was so happy I had done what was right and that He had blessed me with a changed heart, I couldn't stop smiling. The people around me couldn't figure out why I seemed so happy and relieved when I was reporting such bad news. My humble submission to God made all the difference.

These spiritual exercises are sometimes called "holy habits," and their use helps me push aside the things that keep God from making a home in my heart. Their regular practice gives God more and more of me to reshape into the likeness of Christ. Unlike my many failed attempts at confronting my bad habits directly, the disciplines have brought me actual change. Old habits of lying, swearing, and over-work have fallen from me like dead, rotten fruit. And in their place I find fresh new fruit beginning to bloom and grow. This is how we "offer [our] bodies as living sacrifices" and become "holy and pleasing to God" and "do not conform any longer to the pattern of this world" (Romans 12:1-2). I have learned that I must discipline my body to be obedient to the will of God just as Jesus learned obedience (see Hebrews 5:8). The disciplines I practiced incorporated several spiritual disciplines, including examination.

Reflecting on a specific period of time or a specific action and being honest about the degree that you worked with God is called the discipline of examination (journaling is a form of this discipline). Find a particular time to review your day or specific actions. Ask God to illuminate your heart, thoughts, words, and deeds and offer them up to God. This would be when I would admit to God that I had lied. It's important to include the good and bad, your moments of obedience with God's will and times of struggle and separation from Him. Your focus should be on an honest assessment and a humble submission of everything to God. Prayer and fasting can be added to this discipline to help humble your heart and press on to greater honesty and openness. As Richard Foster says in *Celebration of Discipline*, "What freedom corresponds to submission? It is the ability to lay down the terrible burden of always needing to get our own way."[6]

A good example of someone who practiced this was Frank Laubach. In *Man of Prayer*, he records the amount of time he is conscious of God and the level of his surrender to the will of God. On April 8, 1937, he records the following:

Conscious, 75 percent; Surrender, 100 percent

God, last night we crossed the equator. We saw nothing, felt nothing, save the laughter of merrymakers. Yet the equator is a fact in Thy mind and in our minds. And I begged Thee to help me cross an equator of the soul, out of weakness into integration and constant strength, to make this day and the future 100 percent days in surrender. All of them!

God, that crimson, blood-smeared sunset over Africa was Thy call, and I listened to it for half an hour. Africa needs us. God, we have a key to Christ, to hope, to justice. O God, I fear my weak self! Do not let me ever lose that glorious vision.

Thou, Lord, dost talk, and art talking now! This beautiful "Salutation of the Dawn" is Thy eager voice. "Look to this day, for it is life. Today well lived makes every yesterday a dream of happiness. . . ." How happy yesterday leaves me this morning![7]

As you read Laubach's journal entries, you can see the ebb and flow of his relationship to God. You can also see the growing closeness and nearness of God that developed over time. The entries with the highest awareness and surrender are stunning in their expressions of beauty and awe of God and His creation. My experience is similar, and I find not only a freedom from the burden of getting my way and managing outcomes but the sweet closeness of God as I go about my day.

> **PRACTICE·** Set a time that you will review a portion
> of your day. Allow yourself enough time to reflect on
> your heart, activities, thoughts, and feelings with God.
> Practice daily for two weeks.

RIGHT HERE, RIGHT NOW

I just don't think it's possible to separate discipleship from the regular practice of the spiritual disciplines. How do you follow Jesus if you exclude how He lived and focus solely on what He said? Discipleship is a "right-here-right-now" proposition: *In this place, at this time, with God.* And the spiritual disciplines center us in the present moment of God's eternal purpose.

It's fairly easy to detect who's in charge when I talk to people about their work. When I ask them to discuss their job, boss, customers, tasks, and coworkers, I get a clear sense of whether or not Jesus is an integral part of their day. We must make space for God in our lives and learn how to allow Him to fill that space. The disciplines become a receptacle for His grace to work in us and in our lives.

It's not about doctrine or happiness or converting coworkers, however important those things might be. Discipleship is about life, the abundant life that Jesus came to give us (see John 10:10). It's about living fully in God's kingdom and working through all the difficulties and challenges that entails—strained relations with family, friends, enemies, debt, lifestyle decisions, employment. Following Christ is about becoming people who are streams of living water, even at work. It's about performing our jobs thoughtfully, diligently, and in coop-eration with God. It's seeing His supernatural hand in what we are doing together. Loving God is about transforming work into a place of discipleship and loving service to others. It's about making work an integral part of our life in Christ.

Work is not excluded when Paul writes, "Be on your guard; stand firm in the faith; be men of courage; be strong. Do everything in love" (1 Corinthians 16:13-14). Discipleship is about living every present moment in humble obedience to God. William Law wrote something very telling on the subject:

> Every person when he first applies himself to the exercise of this virtue of humility must, as I said before, consider him-self as a learner, that is to learn something that is contrary to former tempers and habits of mind, and which can only be got by daily and constant practice.
>
> He has not only as much to do as he that has some new art or science to learn, but he has also a great deal to unlearn. He is to forget and lay aside his own spirit, which has been a long while fixing and forming itself; he must forget and depart from abundance of passions and opinions which the fashion, and vogue, and spirit of the world has made natural to him.[8]

We have as much to *unlearn* as to *learn* as disciples of Jesus Christ. I have come to know that the grace-filled exercises of the spiritual dis-ciplines are a way to both learn about the heart of Jesus and unlearn my heart's natural tendencies. There is much against us (our former tempers and habits of mind), but through God's grace we can have confidence in the outcome. Jesus knew that becoming a Christian was an all-or-nothing proposition that should be considered seriously and, once decided, required proper action. We must give everything up to follow Christ. We must willingly and gladly sacrifice our life, every aspect of our self, to be with Him. We must learn how to lay aside our "own spirit, which has been a long while fixing and forming itself." C. S. Lewis explains it this way:

> The Christian way is different: harder, and easier. Christ says, "Give me All. I don't want so much of your time and so much of your money and so much of your work: I want You. I have not come to torment your natural self, but to kill it. No half-measures are any good. I don't want to cut off a branch here and a branch there. I want to have the whole tree down. I don't want to drill the tooth, or crown it, or stop it, but to have it out. Hand over the whole natural self, all the desires which you think innocent as well as the ones you think wicked — the whole outfit. I will give you a new self instead. In fact, I will give you Myself: my own will shall become yours."[9]

By regularly practicing spiritual exercises, we can come before God to learn the humility needed to let Jesus be king over our kingdom. As Henri Nouwen said, "Spiritual disciplines are means to prevent everything in your life from being filled up. It means somewhere you're not occupied, and you're certainly not preoccupied. It means to create that space in which something can happen that you hadn't planned on or counted on."[10]

AIDED BY APPRENTICESHIP

Who teaches you? Whose disciple are you? Honestly. Dallas points out, "One thing is sure: You are somebody's disciple. You learned how to live from somebody else. There are no exceptions to this rule, for human beings are just the kind of creatures that have to learn and keep learning from others how to live."[11]

Being a disciple, apprentice, student, and follower involves obedience and trust. Whatever word we choose to describe our relationship with Jesus, it should include trust, obedience, and leave no part of our life out.

We must believe that our life in Jesus is better than our life without Him. Personal experience is the surest way of moving what we believe from our head to our heart. As Donald Coggan once said: "The journey from head to heart is one of the longest and most difficult that we know." Personal experience shortens the trip. There will be times when we join the man who said, "I do believe; help me overcome my unbelief!" (Mark 9:24), but the regular practice of spiritual disciplines, in their many forms, continually gives us the personal experience to move from head belief to heart belief.

THE "BURDEN" OF BEING CHRISTIAN

I used to think the dourest image in all of Christendom was "take up your cross." The image that would pop into my mind was bleak, bloody, and oppressive. What is Jesus asking us to do when He says, "If anyone would come after me, he must deny himself and take up his cross and follow me" (Matthew 16:24; Mark 8:34; Luke 9:23)? If being yoked to Jesus is "easy and light" and will "bring rest for our souls," how could taking up my cross be so grim? What was I missing? *Hope.* Not the wishful empty optimism of today but solid confidence in divine outcomes that we find in the stories about Abel, Enoch, Noah, Abraham, Isaac, Joseph, Moses, Rahab, Gideon, Barak, Samson, Jephthah, David, Samuel, and the prophets (see Hebrews 11).

Taking up our cross means being caught up by what God is doing in our life and in the world. It means we are fully engaged, committed and focused on God's eternal plan. We willingly make sacrifices in order to accomplish what He calls us to do. Our cross is something that we are so passionate about, something that is so important to us, that our whole life shifts its focus toward accomplishing it. When you look at Jesus and the cross, that's what you see. His whole life was directed toward that cross. When you read about Mother Teresa or Billy Graham or the lives of the Christian martyrs, that's what you see: passionate, committed, focused living. There is great passion and joy and freedom when you know your God-given purpose, and your cross doesn't feel heavy.

A JOURNEY OF TRUST

Trusting Jesus doesn't mean we have all the answers; it means we believe that He does. We can doubt, stumble, and fail in Christ. We don't even have to be right. We just have to trust. As apprentices, we come to a place where we learn to trust Jesus even with our job and career.

In a faculty luncheon at the C. S. Lewis Conference in San Diego, June 21, 2003, Dallas Willard was asked to share his experience on the road to tenure in a secular university. His story is a wonderful example of staying focused on God and following the path Christ intends. He explained that he "had not intended to be a university professor—I just ended up there." Dallas loves literature, writing, and thinking, but he and his wife fully expected to spend their lives in full-time church ministry. During his first year as an associate pastor, however, Dallas became convinced that his teachings were actually a hazard to his listeners. Realizing his lack of knowledge gave him a desire to spend more time studying God and the soul. These are topics philosophers discuss in great depth (at least they were), so he studied philosophy for two years, received a PhD, and was invited to teach at the university the following year:

> The Lord moved me step by step. We were offered a position at
> the University of Southern California, without even applying.
> So you can see it's certainly not due to me.
>
> I decided I would do nothing toward trying to secure

myself or gain advancement. I am very much a literalist in terms of the Bible, "Promotion does not come from the East or the West, it comes from the Lord." So I don't have to do anything about promotion. But what I did was say, "I am going to do the best work I can by God's help," and that meant writing and teaching.

The first two papers I published were each two solid years in writing. They were twelve to fifteen pages long, but they'd probably been rewritten sixty-five times. . . .

I sent an article to Gilbert Ryle, who edited the leading philosophical journal at the time, called *Mind*, and within a week and a half I had a really wonderful letter back from him saying, "We want to publish this."

My view is that, if you are in a good field, you must work on the things that are really central and essential to that field. And you ought to believe that God will enable you to do work in the field that will be a benefit and challenge to everyone. . . . I really challenge you to believe that about yourself, whatever your area of work is. *Not because you are so good, but because God is so great.*

What jumps out at you as you read this account is the humble and growing trust in Jesus. My own trust in Jesus was proven when I stood up for what was right and ended up being let go. Management was demanding that my team continue to work overtime. After a year of hard work, demanding schedules, and great accomplishments, I knew it was time for rest. My team was tired and getting burned out, but the demands wouldn't stop. In fact, more was being requested. I took a stand and made it clear that my team needed a well-deserved rest. Within a month, I was gone. After forty days, I had a new job, close to home, and in those forty days I wrote much of this book. Paul says, "For we are God's fellow workers; you are God's field, God's building" (1 Corinthians 3:9). The blessings and goodness are from

God. We must learn to trust Him, to follow Him and to simply do what's good and right and learn that He is always with us, helping us bear much fruit.

CHAPTER THREE

REDEFINING SUCCESS

We move in a world that, it seems, just constantly harasses us and
distracts us from the purposes that in our heart of hearts we feel we
should be doing. . . . It really is because the standards of success that
are accepted and that people are held to, in the various lines of work,
confuse us about what we're supposed to be doing anyway.
DALLAS WILLARD

What does *success* mean? When we talk about a successful business or person or sending our children to the best schools so they can be successful, what are we talking about? Many people in our society would say that someone is successful if he or she possesses wealth, power, influence, and admiration. Unfortunately, these criteria leave out how to be a *good* person by virtue of being in a chosen industry or profession.

This prevailing definition of success has become *the* goal for individuals and businesses. It drives us and defines our actions and life choices, but without goodness as a part of how we define success, our decisions can have some devastating consequences.

BOB HARDWORKER

Let's take a look at the typical American employee, whom we'll call Bob Hardworker. Bob is an average guy raised with traditional values. The point of doing well in school was to get a good job so he could make good money. Bob's parents worried about what preschool, grade school, high school, and college little Bobby would attend. Bob soon joined his parents in obsessing over his grades and SAT scores. His parents made sure their little boy participated in potentially lucrative and socially enhancing sports and activities. They evaluated his friends and made sure they were the "right" kind. Bob learned his lessons well, and when he graduated university and got his first job in corporate America, he took pains to connect with the "right" people.

Bob had learned that money was the means, and the end, for all the good things in life—and that hard work and social connections were the best way to make more. Money is why Bob works, not because money is important per se, but because you need money to be happy, safe, and accepted . . . successful. Money, and the job that pays it, are Bob's protection from the bad things that can happen in life. Every legal, medical, and life issue can be dealt with if you have enough money.

Upon this foundation, Bob builds his role as father and husband, evaluating his worth in light of what he is able to buy for his loved ones. The measure of Bob is seen in the things that he has provided for his wife and children: a nice house, nice cars, clothes, private schools for the kids, and so on. Work is at the center of Bob's life, the wellspring of his success. It not only provides him with a means to happiness, it defines him. Bob makes sacrifices for his family and often misses school plays, ball games, and dates with his wife because he is "the hardworking provider." He feels good about these sacrifices because they reinforce his self-image as a loving father and husband, and they reflect the very best of who he is. He can't understand why his family complains about his absence from these simple nonpaying activities since they aren't what counts.

So what happens when things go wrong? Suppose Bob's company takes a downturn and begins to lay people off . . . or management announces that benefits will be slashed and wages frozen for the foreseeable future . . . or he gets a new boss and has to prove himself all over again . . . or a coworker with less experience and fewer skills gets promoted above him . . . or he gets a DUI on the way home after just a few drinks with his new boss . . . or he learns his company is being bought out. What happens then?

Bob is in the Danger Zone because how he defines himself is threatened. The center of his being is suddenly at risk. Changes at work rock his world. He is on the verge of breaking—all the tiny fractures in his heart, mind, soul, and relationships have become fissures, and he is spiritually and physically falling apart. In his pain, anguish, fear, and frustration, he begins to lash out. He can just as easily lash out at work as he can at home, and in lashing out he continues the destructive cycle he is in and increases the distance from anyone who cares and could help. The question isn't what would Bob do? The question is what *wouldn't* Bob do? What escape or quick-fix wouldn't he embrace (theft, drugs, alcohol, sex, anger, abuse) to relieve the pain and recapture some feeling of control? Poor Bob.

THE PROBLEM OF PRIDE

There was a time in my life when I was much like Bob. It's a life that's success-oriented and job-centered. It all starts by having the wrong ideas about God, work, money, life, and success. The ideas don't seem wrong at first: Everyone has the same ideas, don't they? I learned them from my parents, by watching the people around me (bosses, fellow employees, friends), and by trying to model successful people. I was in charge and in control. My career was moving right along. I was making good money and spending it on the best things. Work and my career were areas of my life where I didn't need God. I was lost but didn't know it.

Even as my life began to unravel, I was still "in charge and in control." I remember how proud I was of my breaking the $100,000-a-year mark and of my wardrobe—Ferragamo shoes, alligator bill-fold, Armani suits. I also remember the $1,000 per month credit card interest I was paying on the twenty-five credit cards, and the night I worried about making it home because I needed gas and didn't have a credit card without a maxed-out limit. I just needed to make more money, so I got a few consulting jobs. I just needed to bridge this momentary gap, so I took out loans and used new credit cards to pay for my other credit cards. The perfect storm of financial ruin and personal disaster was about to hit, and I kept on thinking I could handle it. That's pride fueled by stupid ideas about life and how men are supposed to take care of everything on their own. It kept God out of my life when I needed Him most.

Pride is such an insidious sin that it seeps into our heart, and once there, it hardens it, causing our ears to close and our eyes to go dim. It taints and distorts all that we do. I agree with St. Augustine and C. S. Lewis, who said that pride is the worst of sins because: (1) by itself it's a sin, (2) it compounds and magnifies the sins we commit, and (3) it taints the good that we attempt to do. They both say that pride, not hate, is the opposite of love because wherever there is pride, love cannot exist.

THE FULLNESS OF CHRIST

Jesus doesn't ask us to be successful. He simply asks us to follow Him and learn from Him how to live and be a good person. While we want to be successful, Jesus wants us to love, trust, and obey Him. The question isn't, how do I become a successful plumber? The question is, how can I learn from Jesus how to be a good person while I'm doing my job?

The missing element in Bob's life wasn't success. And no amount of success or money would fix my broken life. The missing piece was Jesus and the goodness and love that can only be found in Him. Defining success at work as growing in the goodness of Christ is *the* workplace challenge for Christians today. True success is "attaining to the whole measure of the fullness of Christ" (Ephesians 4:13), because the "whole measure" includes our life, which includes our job. Wealth, power, influence, and admiration pale in comparison to the fullness of Christ and life in the kingdom. But our society idolizes and demands worldly success, and we demand it for ourselves.

Jesus said, "You cannot serve both God and Money" (Matthew 6:24; Luke 16:13). It was true then; it's true now. Things haven't changed much in two thousand years—we still have the same challenge. Jesus also said, "For where your treasure is, there your heart will be also" (Matthew 6:21; Luke 12:34). If our definition of success leaves God out, as it often does, then our pursuit of success keeps the goodness of God out of our life.

Another way to view our success is through the eyes of the rich young ruler (see Luke 18:18-23). Put yourself in his shoes, but instead of wealth, substitute your job. We have that choice to make every day. Where is Jesus in our pursuits? How do we respond when Jesus looks us in the eye, asking us to give up our success and come follow Him?

The wealth of the rich young ruler was really baggage that kept him from God. For him it was wealth; for us it might be our success, our job, or status. It's whatever keeps us from fully trusting God. We must surrender ourselves to God with a humble heart and learn to lay down our burden. Otherwise we will be like the rich young ruler, unable to set aside what keeps us from entering God's kingdom. The decision to choose Jesus over anything else is the starting point for a life reborn and remade in the likeness of Jesus Christ. The life that Jesus offers is available now—we don't have to wait. The kingdom of God is available to us now through our trust in Jesus Christ. We can read the stories of changed lives in the New Testament and in the amazing words of Paul, Peter, John, and others as they describe their life in the kingdom. We can gaze back in history and see that down through the ages, simple, common, regular people trusted Jesus with their lives, and their lives were forever changed.

THREE MORE POTENTIAL DANGERS

In addition to *success*, there are three other business concepts that can lead us away from God: *competition*, *loyalty*, and *service*. Just as success can mislead, so can these. None of them is inherently evil; it's when they are apart from God that they become problematic.

Competition in business is considered by many to be healthy and good. Healthy and good because it keeps the market strong, increases employee focus, and ensures the best value for the customer. Rubbish! But, wasn't it Paul who said we should run in such a way that we might gain the prize? Yes he did, but the "prize" is Jesus, and the competing is against our own nature of sin. Competition in business as a good thing is only true if we turn a blind eye to the devastation and distraction it often causes. Companies are attacked and destroyed, jobs lost, careers ruined, monopolies formed, all under the banner of competitive advantage.[1] In contrast, Jesus teaches us to "love your enemies, do good to them, and lend to them without expecting to get anything back" (Luke 6:35).

There are two ways to get ahead or "win" in business: godly and worldly. Godly competition is the kind spoken of by Paul in the verse just mentioned where we "run in such a way as to get the prize" (1 Corinthians 9:24). The prize is Christ Jesus, not beating the other guy. Worldly competition strives to win by eliminating or defeating others. In godly competition we "press on toward the goal to win the prize for which God has called [us] heavenward in Christ Jesus" (Philippians 3:14). In business we "beat out" or "take over" the other guy. Godly competition (*struggle* might be a better word) is *striving for perfection* in your chosen market or field of endeavor. With worldly competition, someone wins and someone loses, so it's better that I win. In business, competition is undertaken so that a monopoly can be achieved or some degree of market dominance and control can be gained. This goal is to ensure that customers pay whatever we charge and accept whatever quality we provide. *Worldly competition goes against the concept of work as a loving community oriented around mutual benefit and support.*

BUSINESS IS NOT WAR

Corporate America has taken competition to an extreme by using war as a model for conducting business. War is a violent philosophy that promotes the use of military strategies and tactics in order to gain victory over our enemies. We are told that the *battle* is over market share and that we must gain a competitive advantage or be eliminated. We use terms like "campaign," "attack a problem," "be aggressive," "outflank," "strategic and tactical plans," "hostile takeover," and "dominate the marketplace." They all reflect this warlike philosophy. To fail at competition is to ensure death and doom.

As one military expert wrote, "War is an act of force, and there are no limitations to the application of that force. Each party goads the other on, triggering an interaction that must, theoretically, lead to extremes."[2] The destructive nature of this attitude in business can be seen in the behavior of companies that view competitors as enemies. Anyone who has gone through a corporate takeover can attest to the victimization and in-fighting that ensues. Once you open the door to unrestrained action, destruction will quickly follow, and no amount of rationalizing will prevent people from being hurt and lives from being destroyed. No one intentionally sets out to dehumanize human beings as a natural consequence of business, but labeling a community of people as "the competition" and setting a course of action to defeat them does exactly that. Holding one group of people in higher esteem than others (shareholders versus employees) has the same effect. Is competition something that Christ calls us to, or did He call us to love our enemies (see Matthew 5:44)?

I was in a staff meeting with my boss, and he had a consultant come in. The consultant handed each of us a deck of cards. On the cards were words or phrases that represented personal qualities and characteristics. We were asked to group them into three categories: Critical, Important, and Desirable. We then took our Important pile and selected the top ten. Our boss had done the same. We then compared our top-ten qualities/characteristics with those of our boss. The differences were striking. The consultant stressed how that showed we weren't a team. I looked at it differently; I saw how we complemented one another. The expectation was that we would all be exactly like our boss. But God made us all unique individuals, and He brings different people together to add our own uniqueness. We are called to view others as precious beings deserving of great care and respect. Any attitude, philosophy, label, or excuse that allows us to see people as less than unique beings made in God's image is a sin before God.

Loving community begins at the most fundamental level of our individual relationships — the day-to-day words and actions that flow between each of us — and broadens to include larger groups and communities of people (departments, unions, committees, and neighbors). Loving community applies between departments within the same company, between a company and its suppliers or customers, and between companies in the same industry or business segment. In other words, our "competitors" are members of the larger community who are also serving God's purpose in the same field of endeavor.

"BUSINESS IS A MATTER OF HUMAN SERVICE"

The following excerpts from the *Fortune* article "Sweet Surrender" describe a business built on the principles of loving community and godly competition (striving for perfection).

Milton Hershey wanted both to pioneer mass-production of chocolate . . . and to create a utopian community. . . .

(A sign on his office wall read, *Business is a matter of human service.*) . . .

Common factory workers living in tidy little houses . . . A 150-acre park in the middle of town where they could have lunch . . . $3 million community center . . .

He refused to advertise . . . But his company grew from $2 million in sales in 1907 . . . to $41 million in 1929. The community grew with it, from a population of 700 . . . to 2,500 by the 1930s. . . . Milton Hershey limited home construction in order to preserve green space. Instead he built miles of trolley lines so workers could commute from neighboring towns. . . .

Though Hershey Chocolates sales dropped 50 percent during the 1930s, Milton Hershey wouldn't lay anyone off.[3]

Milton Hershey understood the nature and purpose of work. He embodied the concept of having business be part of a broader community, and he embodied the concept of success being about "human service." Milton Hershey didn't "compete"; he strove for perfection in his chosen field of endeavor. Striving for perfection seems harder, and it looks like the difficult path, but it's not. It is the "easy yoke" and the most enriching. It's what God wants for us because it requires that we humbly admit we aren't better than everyone else and that we behave accordingly. Left to our own devices, we would rather raise ourselves up on the bodies of those we've defeated than to love and serve them.

Milton Hershey set out to make the best mass-produced milk chocolate possible. His company spent no money on advertising until 1972. He relied upon his customers' word of mouth to grow the business. He put himself and his company in the position of total dependence on God and their good work for any future business and growth. He was intelligent, thoughtful, and caring, and he strove to make the very best chocolate.

Let's compare the effects of striving for perfection versus competition in the areas of market strength, employee focus, and customer value.

Market strength. Increasing a company's value within its field. Striving for perfection will enhance company value by directing greater effort and attention to the company's actual business—product quality and service excellence within their market. Competition will diminish a company's value by wasting effort on competing with others instead of on improving core company products and services. Competition could take the form of attacks against a competitor's website, unfounded lawsuits, false advertising, and similar activities that distract from a company's value to the community.

Employee focus. Every company wants its employees focused on the right things. Striving for perfection holds every job to be valuable because they all support the goal of the company to meet the needs of its customers. Employees are more connected to the mission of the company, are more focused, and can see their role in benefiting others. Competition, on the other hand, puts the focus not on the value the company brings but on market share by any means. Without a real sense of how their job matters to the company and the community it serves, employees are more apt to be out for themselves. One real sign of this is the degree of corporate espionage that takes place in the world today.

Customer value. Ensuring that each customer is honored, respected, and valued by providing the best quality product or service. Striving for perfection will increase customer loyalty because the company focus will be on meeting customers' needs through product quality and service excellence. Competition will diminish customer value because it will treat the customer as a statistic and a source of revenue, and we will lose sight of the customer as a human being and overlook the customer's actual need. Should the focus of a company be on the product or service quality or on the number of customers and profit? When you are buying a parachute or pacemaker or tires, where do you want the company focus?

WHAT'S WRONG WITH LOYALTY?

If you polled every culture and asked for the top ten virtues, loyalty would likely be on every list. No one questions the importance and benefit of loyalty and rightly so. The problem comes when loyalty trumps truth.[4] In 2002, *Time* magazine's "Persons of the Year" were Cynthia Cooper, Coleen Rowley, and Sherron Watkins. These women understood the importance of individual responsibility (truth) within a corporate community that demanded loyalty. All three took personal and professional risks to tell the truth and right wrongs within their communities: Cynthia Cooper at WorldCom, the company that over-stated its earnings by $9 billion; Coleen Rowley at the FBI, regarding pre-9/11 terrorist activities; and Enron's Sherron Watkins, who alerted Kenneth Lay about accounting irregularities. They are three people who, in their own words, were trying to fix the organizations they worked for from within. As the *Time* article put it, they were "ever faithful to the idea that where they worked was a place that served the wider world in some important way."[5]

Their stories help us see the dangers and conflicts inherent in truth when it goes against the expectation of unswerving allegiance (loyalty). Mrs. Watkins said, "There were some very bleak moments throughout when you're just so disappointed with human nature, with the power of greed and the power of denial, trying to rationalize that you've done nothing wrong." I don't know a single person who hasn't faced a similar situation. As Christians, we are called to "serve wholeheartedly, as if you were serving the Lord" (Ephesians 6:7). And we are called to resist evil by struggling "against the rulers, against the authorities, against the powers of this dark world" (Ephesians 6:12). That puts us right in the middle of this truth-versus-loyalty dilemma. It helps that between those two verses is, "Be strong in the Lord and in his mighty power" (6:10). It's not an easy task to know when to be loyal to your company because of the good it does and when to resist the evil you find within. That's where Jesus comes in. That's where discipleship and the disciplines make a profound difference. To imagine that we can stand in the middle and mediate between loyalty and truth—to have one foot in a world that forsakes people for money and one foot in the kingdom of God—is to succumb to a dangerous double-minded kind of blindness that allows us to compromise our beliefs and dishonor God.

Jesus gives us the clear message of choice, "No one can serve two masters" (Matthew 6:24). And "He will put the sheep on his right and the goats on his left" (Matthew 25:33). We have to choose God or money, be a sheep or a goat, there is no third choice. When it comes to a choice of truth versus loyalty, we must honor truth and trust God. Compromise is not an option, there is no moderately good tree with mediocre fruit in the kingdom of God. Compromise only means we are trying to live our religion from our head not our heart, and negotiating our way through life as the Pharisees did with external compliance (see Matthew 23). They loved manipulating their religion as a means of managing truth and proclaiming, "I did nothing wrong."

We must live our lives with both feet firmly planted in the abundant, eternal, and powerful kingdom of God. And we must arm ourselves with truth, righteousness, peace, salvation, and the power to stand firm (see Ephesians 6:10-18). Nothing else is strong enough to withstand the pressures of this world. We must each become a light in our world, accepting the responsibility of doing what is good and right and honoring truth in the face of worldly pressures and perceived disloyalty.

PRACTICE TAKING RESPONSIBILITY

The sin of omission can often be more damning than the sin of commission (such as the rich man and Lazarus from Luke 16:19-31). In like manner, nonparticipation in rumors, off-color jokes, knowing glances, or comments can help positively change the tone in a workplace by limiting evil's fuel supply. We also know the don'ts like stealing, coveting, and doing personal work on company time. But sometimes we must take a stand, fill the gap, and do what's right, no matter the cost. Paul pointed to this when he wrote, "Have nothing to do with the fruitless deeds of darkness, but rather expose them" (Ephesians 5:11).

Do you recall the Old Testament story of Esther? She is someone, just like you, who finds herself exactly where God wants her to be, but not where *she* would have chosen. She is favored by the king, who doesn't know that she is Jewish, and is selected as queen. She soon learns of an evil plot that will destroy her people. She knows only the king can save her people, but there is an edict that anyone who comes before the king uninvited will be killed, including her. Confused and frightened, she sends a request to her uncle, Mordecai, for advice on what she should do:

> When Esther's words were reported to Mordecai, he sent back this answer: "Do not think that because you are in the king's house you alone of all the Jews will escape. For if you remain silent at this time, relief and deliverance for the Jews will arise from another place, but you and your father's family will perish. And who knows but that you have come to royal position for such a time as this?"
>
> Then Esther sent this reply to Mordecai: "Go, gather together all the Jews who are in Susa, and fast for me. Do not eat or drink for three days, night or day. I and my maids will fast as you do. When this is done, I will go to the king, even though it is against the law. And if I perish, I perish." (Esther 4:13-17)

Esther stood in the gap. She had no assurance that she would survive, but she chose to risk her life and leave the outcome to God. She did one thing we don't normally do—she prepared spiritually and asked those around her to do the same. She focused her entire circle of influence on the event.

This is the only spiritual discipline that we can't easily schedule, but the opportunity to exercise responsibility for doing what is right occurs frequently enough. This is where we go from practicing the spiritual disciplines to putting them *into* practice. They are no longer being practiced; they are being performed.

> **PRACTICE·** Put this spiritual discipline into practice
> by asking family, friends, coworkers, and your church to
> fast and pray (at least pray) for an important decision or
> event in your life. Do what is right, no matter the feared
> outcome. The spiritual disciplines are exercises for what is
> to come.

THE CUSTOMER SERVICE TRAP

Success, competition, loyalty—service is the final area of confusion and challenge. Everyone in business is focused on customer service, which today means giving customers what they want even if it isn't what's best for them. In the kingdom of God, service is rooted in love. But what does it mean to love someone? It means that we *will their good*. We invest ourselves in things that are best for them, so our focus is on what they *need*. That sometimes brings us into conflict with what they *want*. As a parent, I am often confronted with my children wanting something that isn't good for them (excess candy, TV, and staying up late, just to name a few). Since I love them and seek their good, I interfere with their desires and try to direct them in ways that are good for them. I am willing to sacrifice their present opinion of me in order to do what is good for them.

At work, I am presented with similar challenges. All of us are. People I work with (subordinates, peers, supervisors, customers, vendors) desire something, and they expect me to give it to them. However, my understanding of what is good for them might be different from their expectation. This gap can account for a great deal of friction and politicking in the workplace, as people seek to get what they want and refuse to accept anything else. Am I willing to sacrifice their present opinion of me (and possibly my job) in order to accomplish what is best for them?

In our society, many people find themselves in moral and ethical quandaries: fast-food workers who know that much of the food they dispense is unhealthy; advertising specialists who promote products that are environmentally damaging or completely wasteful; pharmacists and physicians who give medications that only mask deeper problems; bankers and credit-company employees whose loans sink people deeper into debt . . . the list is endless, and so are the moral and ethical questions. And in the middle of it all are people like you and me, trying to make a living, doing what we can to provide for ourselves and our families, striving to do a good day's work. Lots of questions and one answer—trust Jesus. He has the answers to life's questions, and He will guide us and lead us into making the right decisions and living a full life.

There are thousands of challenging examples, but let's look at something simple we all do to provide a loving service: conversation. Our everyday conversations can be an uplifting service to others and proclaim God's kingdom. As Ephesians 4:29 tells us, "Do not let any unwholesome talk come out of your mouths, but only what is helpful for building others up according to their needs, that it may benefit those who listen." Don't swear, lie, or gossip but talk about good things, build people up, be aware of their needs. This is different from saying what people want to hear because it also includes helping them in a loving way to see their faults and ways that they can improve and grow. It's working out the details in our jobs of how to love others by "speaking the truth in love" so we can "grow up into him who is the Head, that is, Christ" (Ephesians 4:15). Talking is one simple and powerful way that we can, under any circumstance, be a servant to others and serve them well.

I remember when a coworker said, "Bill, I wonder if I can ask you a question."

I assured her that she could.

"How do you stay so calm?" she asked. "In the midst of all this tension and friction, how do you do it?"

I told her I had an eternal perspective, respected the people I was working with, believed they were doing their best, and had confidence that things would work out. Months later, she came to me asking for advice about her son, who was having trouble. Ultimately, these conversations led her to decide to change careers and be at home raising her children and caring for her husband.

"YA DIG SIXTEEN TONS . . ."

The distorted ideas about success, competition, loyalty, and service combine with greed to make the workplace a tough dehumanizing environment. Add in a dash of worry, a cup of stress, two teaspoons of tired, and bake in the oven of "every man for himself" for a few years, and you can see why things are the way they are. It can be truthfully said that things are getting worse. Every day we can pick up a newspaper and read about the brokenness of work. Ten years ago, the U.S. Department of Labor's Occupational Safety and Health Administration (OSHA) had to begin tracking workplace violence as a distinct category of death and injury on the job. We read about how work through greed, neglect, and arrogance hurts and injures people physically, financially, and spiritually. Dallas Willard and C. S. Lewis give us insight into the moral direction our society is taking and its effect on each of us. Although they address the societal conditions in general, work and society are inseparable.

Willard:

Lust and pride all around us inevitably result in a world of fear. For they bring us into a world of little dictators; and the most likely thing is that each person will be used and abused by others, possibly destroyed, and at least not helped and cared for. Our families, which should be a refuge from such a world, often turn out to be places where victimization is at its worst. . . . Injury brings pain and loss, then fear and anger, which mingle with resentment and contempt and settle into postures of coldness and malice, with brutal feelings that drain the body of health and strength and shatter social well-being.[6]

Lewis:

When I have started a sum the wrong way, the sooner I admit this and go back and start over again, the faster I shall get on. There is nothing progressive about being pigheaded and refusing to admit a mistake. And I think if you look at the present state of the world, it is pretty plain that humanity has been making some big mistake. We are on the wrong road. And if that is so, we must go back. Going back is the quickest way on.[7]

This is not what God intended! These conditions speak to a growing sense of hopelessness, loss, and hurt, which lies at the root of the anger and destruction we find in workplace violence. In 1990, Lee Hardy discussed this same problem in his book *The Fabric of This World* when he wrote about "the great moral problem of the modern age":

Working men have been given over, isolated and defenseless, to the callousness of employers and the greed of unrestrained competition. . . . The moral problem encompassed not only the material deprivation of the workers, but also the dehabilitating spiritual effect of modern methods of production upon the human soul. Labor, which was originally given for man's good, Pope Pius XI noted with sad irony, "has everywhere been changed into an instrument of strange perversion: for dead matter leaves the factory ennobled and transformed, where men are corrupted and degraded."[8]

The world desperately needs the good news of Jesus Christ embodied in everyday Christian workers, not by having Scripture quoted but by having it lived out. We must learn Christ (not just learn *about* Christ) in how we work. We must learn how to stand in the gap and be strong and loving in the face of all the pressures that swirl and press upon us. The joy of living comes from meeting these circumstances with God, knowing that He is always with us. We stand firm upon the rock of Christ Jesus in the midst of the storm, waiting for the wind, earthquake, and fire to pass by so we can hear the gentle whisper of God's voice saying, "Well done, good and faithful servant."

TRUST IN THE LORD

Instead of success, we seek to be good. Instead of competing, we strive for perfection. We live in truth and work unto the Lord. Our service springs forth from the assurance and abundance of God's love. All of these radical changes require a firm foundation of trust in the Lord. Jesus says, "Do not worry about your life, what you will eat or drink; or about your body, what you will wear" (Matthew 6:25). Instead of worrying about clothing, food, and our body, Jesus tells us to "seek first his kingdom and his righteousness, and all these things will be given to you as well" (Matthew 6:33). Each of us is prompted to ask himself: Whom do you follow, whom do you trust, from where do you draw your strength?

The writer of Hebrews said, "Let us throw off everything that hinders and the sin that so easily entangles" (12:1). It isn't enough to avoid sin; we must get rid of whatever keeps us from doing God's will so we can fully participate in His kingdom and His righteousness. We learn to trust God more as we live more and more of our life in His care. Nothing is more valuable than a wealth of experience (knowledge) in the awesome power of God. To see more of His hand in the world around us and discover Him even in the most difficult and stressful situations is to learn how to find true rest. As Peter wrote, "For if you possess these qualities in increasing measure, they will keep you from being ineffective and unproductive in your knowledge of our Lord Jesus Christ" (2 Peter 1:8).

SHE WASN'T ALWAYS MOTHER TERESA

Before Agnes Gonxha Bojaxhiu became known as Mother Teresa, she went to Darjeeling, India as a novice, and God spoke to her heart. As she puts it, she found a calling within a calling. Her career led her to Calcutta, a place of great need, and as she looked at the suffering masses all around her, she discovered that God had a plan for her. Today, we view Mother Teresa in the light of all that she accomplished, but we must look at her decision in the midst of that great need—before she was Mother Teresa. She did what needed doing and sought God in all she did.

The needs are right where we are. "The poor you will always have with you," Jesus said (Mark 14:7). Many of the needy are right where we work, many of the most needy are people we work with. Mother Teresa would often say to people seeking to help her mission, "Your help is needed at home." Just as Mother Teresa found a calling within a calling, so we should look around and see how we can be of loving service to others. It is in *this place* and at *this time* that we will find those that God intends us to serve. Mother Teresa didn't set out to be "Mother Teresa" and to help the poor and dying untouchables of India. She found herself there as part of her job and blossomed by meeting the needs of those around her. In her Nobel Peace Prize acceptance speech, she quoted the prayer of Saint Francis:

Lord, make me a channel of Thy peace.
That, where there is hatred, I may bring love,
That, where there is wrong, I may bring the spirit of forgiveness,
That, where there is discord, I may bring harmony;
That, where there is error, I may bring truth;
That, where there is doubt, I may bring faith;

That, where there is despair, I may bring hope;
That, where there are shadows, I may bring light;
That, where there is sadness, I may bring joy.

Lord, grant that I may seek rather to comfort than to be
    comforted,
To understand than to be understood;
To love than to be loved;
For it is by forgetting self that one finds;
It is by forgiving that one is forgiven;
It is by dying that one awakens to eternal life.

Mother Teresa also said something that embodies this life of servanthood from a heart of love, gentleness, and humility:

There is so much suffering, so much hatred, so much misery, and we with our prayer, with our sacrifice are beginning at home. Love begins at home, and it is not how much we do, but how much love we put in the action that we do. It is to God Almighty — how much we do it does not matter, because He is infinite, but how much love we put in that action. How much we do to Him in the person that we are serving.[9]

Love is what matters. It doesn't matter the amount of action that we take but the amount of love that we put into our actions toward others. Read 1 Peter 4:8-11 and compare it to the life of Mother Teresa. Can you see her heart and life reflected in this passage? It isn't the life of Mother Teresa that we should pursue, but our life given over to Christ — to find Jesus wherever we are and serve Him in whatever we do. When we become reborn, become more the self that God intended, we will find true success.

CHAPTER FOUR

YOU ARE HERE: GOD AS OUR REFERENCE POINT

To each of us is given a garden. It is our life. God gives us all the grace and wisdom we will need if we will cultivate it under Him. And when we do, wherever we are in life, God will be there.

DALLAS WILLARD

Do you ever wonder how those maps at the mall know exactly where you are? It's amazing. They always know that, "You are here," right outside Sears! But what if we put that exact mall map on a tree in Yosemite? Can a map help if you are *really* lost? Nope! If you're truly lost, you can't even find yourself on a map. Someone trying to help you would ask, "Where are you?" and you would answer, "I have no idea."

When your life is "lost," it means you have no idea where you are or where to go. The rich young ruler was lost. He was at a cross-road and didn't know it. He had two paths to choose from—money or God—and he chose money.

You have two paths for your life, the world's and God's. Following the world's map means money is your goal and giving all your time to work is the path. Following Jesus means God is at the center of your life and your path is brightly lit by love and grace and Jesus. God's character and power pulsate around you. You live a full life following Jesus (see John 10:10). As Jesus said, "I am the way and the truth and the life" (John 14:6).

A coworker came and asked to speak with me. She said she wanted advice about her son, who had autism. She wanted to know if she should quit her job to take care of him or continue to work and pay for private schooling. Over the course of several weeks, we talked and prayed about her dilemma. Amazingly, God charted a path for her that allowed her to be at home with her son and work a part-time job that helped meet their financial needs. She found her answer because work is a place of loving community.

With God at the center of our lives, we know where we are and where we are going (we have our moral compass). No matter what our condition—happy or sad, rich or poor, healthy or sick, young or old—we are never lost. With our eyes fixed upon Jesus, we know where we are going. We don't do it alone. We journey with others, and in community we journey as God intended. In *Mere Christianity*, C. S. Lewis uses a naval convoy as a helpful metaphor to describe our individual and community responsibilities in how we travel and in the shared vision of where we are going. The individual ships must be in good working order, with a competent captain. The ships work together and must be in right relationship with one another, doing their assigned tasks. The whole fleet must know where it's going (or at least trust who is leading them) and how they plan on getting there.[1] The convoy has a leader (an admiral) who guides them with wisdom, knowledge, and skill. No matter how complex or dangerous circumstances might become, he knows what to do. This concept is embodied in the word *righteousness* and in the traditional understanding of morals and ethics. They all begin with a center of goodness, in the individual and within the society, and that center is God.

Without God as the point of reference we, as individuals and collectively, are lost and confused. Individually, we won't know where to go or what to do — we run into each other. And as a society, we mill around or try to move in a thousand directions at once.

Being in right relationship with God and others (righteousness) is crucial to our walk and especially important at work. With God at the center we can help bring order out of chaos. Moving with purpose, clarity, and passion often helps to give people hope and direction. With God as our point of reference, the center of our life, the world looks and feels very different. When God is at the center of all things, great good can be accomplished. One example of this is the formation and early period of the United States of America. God's love as expressed in His Son Jesus Christ was foundational in everything that our founding fathers created for the benefit of future generations — the Declaration of Independence, the Bill of Rights, the system of checks and balances among the three branches of our democratic government. The inalienable rights that Thomas Jefferson wrote into the Declaration were given to all men from our Creator, God. In 1776, Patrick Henry wrote, "It cannot be emphasized too strongly or too often that this great Nation was founded not by religionists, but by Christians; not on religions, but on the Gospel of Jesus Christ. For that reason alone, people of other faiths have been afforded freedom of worship here."

In the same way, believing in a loving, powerful, and active God changes how you work with other people. Life becomes a wondrous place full of God's love. Knowing that we are unceasing spiritual beings with an eternal destiny in God's great universe gives us knowledge about who we are and who we are working with.[2] It is this "center" of goodness that has guided those who have created businesses and organizations that are "streams of water in the desert and the shadow of a great rock in a thirsty land" (Isaiah 32:2). Organizations such as the Christian Legal Society, Write On, St. Thomas University School of Law, ServiceMaster, and others strive to chart a better course within their respective industries and society as a whole.[3]

TIMELESS WISDOM FROM A GODLY FATHER

A shining example of the goodness that can spring forth from having God at the center of your life and career is found in the professional accomplishments of former UCLA basketball coach John Wooden. He is widely regarded as the greatest college coach (of any sport) in history. During his tenure with the Bruins, Wooden became known as the "Wizard of Westwood" and gained lasting fame by winning 665 games in twenty-seven seasons and ten NCAA titles during his last twelve seasons, including seven in a row from 1967 to 1973. His UCLA teams also had a record-winning streak of eighty-eight games, four perfect 30-0 seasons, and won thirty-eight straight games in NCAA Tournaments.

Coach Wooden credits his father with his beliefs about life and how to strive to be the best. John Wooden taught the members of his teams how to be good people both on and off the court. He taught them how to strive for perfection in everything they did and that success comes from knowing you made the effort to become the best you are capable of becoming. He has distilled his philosophy into the John Wooden "Pyramid of Success."

PYRAMID OF SUCCESS

COMPETITIVE GREATNESS
"Perform at your best when your best is required. Your best is required each day."

POISE
"Be yourself. Don't be thrown off by events whether good or bad."

CONFIDENCE
"The strongest steel is well-founded self-belief. It is earned, not given."

CONDITION
"Ability may get you to the top, but character keeps you there — mental, moral, and physical."

SKILL
"What a leader learns after you've learned it all counts most."

TEAM SPIRIT
"The star of the team is the team. 'We' supercedes 'me'."

SELF-CONTROL
"Control of your organization begins with control of yourself. Be disciplined."

ALERTNESS
"Constantly be aware and observing. Always seek to improve yourself and the team."

INITIATIVE
"Make a decision! Failure to act is often the biggest failure of all."

INTENTNESS
"Stay the course. When thwarted try again; harder; smarter. Persevere relentlessly."

INDUSTRIOUSNESS
"Success travels in the company of very hard work. There is no trick, no easy way."

FRIENDSHIP
"Strive to build a team filled with camaraderie and respect: comrades-in-arms."

LOYALTY
"Be true to yourself. Be true to those you lead."

COOPERATION
"Have utmost concern for what's right rather than who's right."

ENTHUSIASM
"Your energy and enjoyment, drive and dedication will stimulate and greatly inspire others."

www.CoachJohnWooden.com
Used by permission.

I recently had an opportunity to use this example at work. My new organization wanted to spend time on our team characteristics. I presented the Pyramid of Success, and it has influenced how we are thinking and talking about work and what it means to be a team. I would recommend that you spend some time reading through each of the "blocks" of the pyramid at www.coachjohnwooden.com. Here's a taste of what he says about cooperation: "In order to reach the full potential of the group, there must be Cooperation at all levels—working together in all ways to accomplish the common goal. And to get Cooperation, you must give Cooperation. You are not the only person with good ideas. If you wish to be heard, listen. Always seek to find the best way rather than insisting on your own way."[4] He also has a seven-point creed that is brimming with godly wisdom. Point 4: Drink deeply from good books—especially the Bible. Point 6: Build shelter against a rainy day (faith in God). Point 7: Pray for guidance and counsel and give thanks for your blessings each day.

Within the community of his family, Coach Wooden learned from his father not only how to be a good person but how to do it within a community of people, and how to teach others to pursue success in one's chosen endeavor. God is the foundation, His love infuses itself into each block, and it is to His glory and the benefit of others that we strive to be the best we can be.

FRAMEWORK OF FAITH

Coach Wooden built a structure or framework for his players to pursue success. When we look around at all that God has created, we see His structures for us to live full and eternal lives. These are loving structures that God has provided to help guide and nurture us on our journey with Him. The prayer of St. Patrick's breastplate offers another way to think about the framework God has designed for us:

Christ before me, Christ behind me,
Christ in me, Christ beneath me, Christ above me,

Christ on my right, Christ on my left,
Christ when I lie down, Christ when I sit down, Christ when
    I arise.

God made the heavens and the earth, the sun, moon, and stars, the lands and seas, the seasons, the flora and fauna, for us. He made time and space and the natural laws that operate in our universe (motion, gravity). He made color and light, darkness and texture, smells and sensations. He gave us reason and understanding. He created men and women in His image, marriage, family, community, work, laughter, tears, desires, and talents. Trust in God allows us to see and experience all of these structures that He lovingly made for us as loving structures in His kingdom made for our blessing and benefit. Within them we can find and experience God.

OTHER STRUCTURES OF LOVE IN THE KINGDOM

With the loving structure of *time and space*, God has provided us with a means of dealing with events in our lives in a sequential manner—one thing at a time and in the present moment of God's eternal purpose. Every day is fresh and new. Our bodies provide us with a source of relatively independent power. We have the ability to decide what to do and can choose to submit to God's will. Being obedient to God and seeking His ways allows our life to be a wellspring of His character and power and allows us to extend His qualities to those around us. The refreshing nature of days, weeks, months, and seasons provides us with new beginnings, clear endings, seasonal planning, and periods of Sabbath rest and Jubilee. Marriage, family, friends, and work provide us with loving community structures where we can rest, play, live, laugh, learn, love, work, and give. Our heart, mind, soul, and body are nourished and refreshed and we, in turn, do the same for others.

Work is the extension of the loving structure of family that gives us the framework in which to share our skills with others and have our own needs met in the process. Within these communities (family, church, friendship, and work), our unique talents, desires, and gifts can blossom and flourish and our purpose in God's kingdom can be fulfilled. We find our place on God's map, and we know where we are going and how to get there.

Realizing the loving nature of God and His creation changes us by opening our hearts to His love and truth. It rekindles the wonder and amazement of our youth. Sunrises, sunsets, music, the patterns of leaves, the workings of your hand, the rain and snow, the stars in the heavens all become wondrous again. The creativity, human value, and participation in meeting needs bring joy that can thrive within the structure of work and be made new each day. Without this vision and understanding of God's loving structures, they can become monotonous, dull, utter drudgery, and great burdens. We can find ourselves drowning in hopelessness instead of overflowing with joy. Malachi 4:2 tells us, "But for you who revere my name, the sun of righteousness will rise with healing in its wings. And you will go out and leap like calves released from the stall." Imagine feeling this way about work! Only a heart that seeks and comes to know God's abundant love is able to make work a place of loving community.

DAILY BREAD: BLESSING OTHERS AT WORK

In his book *The Fabric of This World*, Lee Hardy brings focus to work as a loving structure:

> Having fashioned a world filled with resources and potentials, God chose to continue his creative activity in this world through the work of human hands. In his commentary on Genesis, Luther claims that God even milks the cows through those called to that work. Through our work, humble though it may be, people are being brought under God's providential

care. For God established the various stations of earthly life as channels for his love and providence for the human race; when people respond to the duties of those stations in the activity of work, God is present as the one who provides us with all that we need. With persons as his hands and co-workers God gives his gifts through the earthly vocations, towards man's life on earth (food through farmers and fishermen; external peace through princes, judges, and orderly powers; knowledge and education through teachers and parents . . .). As we pray each morning for our daily bread, people are already busy at work in the bakeries.[5]

We are God's hands, His buildings, fields, and fellow workers in this world, and He created us to love Him and others. We pray for our daily bread and our prayers are answered when the hands of many unknown people perform the simple tasks of everyday work. We are a part of that, both in the asking and in the doing. We are the chosen daily means through which our loving Father provides for the needs of all His children.

Think about all that goes into baking bread. It's not just the baker who bakes the bread. Scientists help to ensure the ingredients are healthy, nutritious, and plentiful. Farmers plant and harvest the wheat. Manufacturers make and maintain the machines that plant, harvest, and process the wheat. People in public service ensure the infrastructure — roads, railways, airways, and shipping lanes — is able to bring ingredients to market (and don't forget the people who pay the taxes to support those efforts). The delivery people, the packagers, the storekeepers, the stock people, the grocery clerks, the baggers, the people that manufacture the cars, buses, and bicycles that help us bring the bread home, the people who make the refrigerators, plastic bags, knives, and plates that we use when we serve the bread — all of them are part of God's fulfilling our prayer for daily bread. And it isn't just bread but all our daily needs for food, water, clothing, shelter, justice, mercy, healing, joy, comfort, and more. Every day, whether we see the loving nature of work or not, we contribute to fulfilling "daily bread" prayers.

In the warmth and aroma of a simple loaf of bread, we see a thriving community of people who are brought together to meet other people's needs. Lee Hardy's book reminds us about the connectedness we have with one another, the threads of action that bind us together. These are threads woven together into a fabric that supports, comforts, and nurtures us all. We are all dependent upon God and each other. We have much to learn about life and how to work in His kingdom and be a part of His plan for our lives. As Dallas Willard emphasizes:

> To take His yoke means joining Him in His work, making our work His work. To trust Him is to understand that total immersion in what He is doing with our life is the best thing that could ever happen to us.
>
> If I am a plumber, clerk, bank manager, homemaker, elected official, senior citizen, or migrant worker, I am in "full-time" Christian service no less than someone who earns his or her living in a specifically religious role. Jesus stands beside me and teaches me in all I do to live in God's world. He shows me how, in every circumstance, to reside in His Word and thus be a genuine apprentice of His—His disciple indeed. This enables me to find the reality of God's world everywhere I may be, and thereby to escape from enslavement to sin and evil (John 8:31-32). We become able to do what we know to be good and right, even when it is humanly impossible. Our lives and words become constant testimony of the reality of God.[6]

THE FRUITS OF FASTING

Jesus taught us how to fast (see Matthew 6:16-18) and reminds us how joyful and important it is to do so. He taught us to put food into its proper perspective (see Matthew 6:25) and knew from experience that Satan would use it to tempt (see Luke 4:3-4). He lived with the understanding that the Word and will of God is more important and nourishing than food (see John 4:34). Fasting is also important because it helps us get to the root of our beliefs about our spiritual nature and our physical nature. Are they different things or different aspects of the same thing? We can't live by bread alone; we need God as well. Fasting (full or partial), regularly practiced, gives us a core ability to say no to our feelings and yes to God. As Dallas points out when he teaches on this subject, "The main role of fasting is to learn how to access and live by the energy of God, rather than deriving our energy from food. It is a way of being dependent on God—whereas fullness is a way of being independent."[7] And as Jeremy Taylor says, "Fasting is not to be commended as a duty, but as an instrument. It is called the nourishment of prayer, the restraint of lust, the wings of the souls, the diet of angels, the instrument of humility and self-denial; the purification of the spirit."[8]

I have found that when I fast, I am more alert, I have more energy and creativity, and my relationships with people are more connected. I have found that my activities are more fruitful (sometimes in amazing ways!) when I have fasted beforehand. There is a lightness to my thoughts, better clarity, less distraction ("God things" tend to happen). I remember going out to lunch with two coworkers on a day that I was fasting (this means I was stretching my legs and getting something to drink). They asked why I wasn't eating, and I told them I was fasting. They asked why and I said, "To draw closer to God." Knowing that their religious traditions included fasting (one was Muslim and the other Hindu), I asked them why they fasted. They said, "Tradition." Once they got over the fact that I wasn't doing it for any other reason, we had a lively and meaningful conversation about fasting, religion, and faith.

I am still growing in this discipline, but I find God's blessing even when I set aside just one meal. The other blessing I receive is rediscovering how much better food tastes and the enjoyment of eating the food God has provided me. We have food so readily available to us that we forget how grateful we should be for it. In so many ways, the little that I set aside is magnified a hundredfold in what I receive back from God.

> **PRACTICE·** Start small—don't hurt yourself. Plan to do without a particular food or meal, and whenever the desire or hunger pang shows up, offer it up to God. Be intentional. Select an important event or a particular day and fast just prior to and throughout it. Evaluate what happens. The goal is to get to a place where you are doing something while fasting and not constantly thinking, *I'm fasting.*

WRAPPED IN PRAYER

Fasting is not complete without prayer—in fact, nothing is complete without prayer. Frank Laubach said to "precede, enfold and follow all deeds with prayer. Prayer and action should be wedded."[9] By praying simple prayers before and after an event or task, I "wrap" it in prayer. When going through my e-mail, I read each message and then say a small prayer before I reply. The prayer will differ based on the e-mail, but I ask God to be with me when I respond. After I've sent the e-mail, I thank God for the opportunity to work with Him and pray for His kingdom to be made manifest.

This practice has been fruitful in several ways: (1) I have taken the most mundane task at work and made it part of what God and I are doing together; (2) I write better e-mails and get some amazing responses and results; (3) I have become more aware of His presence and action in my life; (4) it has enhanced my conversational relationship with Him; (5) I am able to see His hand in more and more places because I have learned to look for Him in the smallest of things; and (6) I have learned that in the smallest details of my job, God is there if I ask Him in. Prayer is one way to invite God in and receive His blessing. He blesses the activity, and I joyfully look for the results of His hand in our shared efforts.

> **PRACTICE·** Pick a task, large or small, and wrap it in prayer. Do this consistently for one week.

JESUS, THE SMARTEST PERSON YOU KNOW

When I talk to fellow Christians, I frequently find that Jesus plays a limited role in their actual work. This isn't intentional — they love Jesus and mean to follow Him, but they only look to Him for "spiritual" help, however they define that. They understand that they need to be good people in how they behave at work just as they would elsewhere, but they don't think of Jesus as having the knowledge necessary to help them. What does Jesus know about business, programming computers, measuring amplitude, fixing electric motors, arc welding, or anything else we find in the modern workplace? People look somewhat confused when I ask, "What does Jesus know about your job?" They never thought to ask Jesus for help with the details of their job.

Do we consider Jesus to be the smartest person in our field? I work in the computer field, and the list of people who tell me they have the knowledge that I need to do my job is overwhelming. From experience I can tell you that no one can write a program, run a meeting, plan a project, or teach a class better than Jesus.

It's impossible to wholeheartedly and unreservedly follow someone who is adequate only in certain areas. We naturally follow people we believe are the experts. We don't follow leaders — take their advice, respect their wisdom, and devote ourselves to their instruction — unless we are fully confident in their expertise.

Simply stated, there is no job where Jesus is not *the* expert.

Let's review a few things. Jesus has control of everything; He is the author of life, and everything is under Him. Because He understands reality at its most fundamental level, He was able to feed five thousand people with just a few loaves and fish (my wife wants that recipe); He was able to walk on water, heal (not just fix) all types of sickness and physical deformity, even raise a dead man after four days in the grave. The list of His abilities goes on and on. At some point, we need to fully grasp that when we call Him Lord of *all*, it includes our job. If He can change water into wine, He can certainly understand computers and motors and TVs and electricity and iPods. That part of our life where we don't consider Jesus as the expert is exactly the part of our life where we aren't His disciple. What part of your life are you willing to leave out?

HE'S RIGHT BESIDE US

The great Christian leader and Holocaust survivor Corrie ten Boom understood this principle. She knew Jesus as an expert watchmaker who was available to help her as she worked in her father's watch shop. She wrote:

> When my hand was not steady and I had to do a very exact work of putting a frail part of a watch — the balance, for instance — into the movement, I prayed, "Lord Jesus, will You lay Your hand on my hand?" He always did, and our joined hands worked securely. Jesus never fails us for a moment. I experienced the miracle that the highest potential of God's love and power is available to us in the trivial things of everyday life.[10]

When we work in God's kingdom, we are a fellow worker with Him. The image of Him standing right beside us, helping us perform our tasks, and watching us learn and grow is a vision that will nurture our hearts and minds. God is always with us, always waiting to join His hand with ours. He is right there, where we are, working with us to accomplish the task before us, whatever that task might be. We should expect to see the results of His supernatural workmanship in what we have done together.

Corrie ten Boom learned to live as a disciple of Christ from her father, who repaired and sold watches. Her early life was filled with examples of living a life that included God in every aspect. Because of her faithfulness in turning to God regularly throughout each day, she was able to carry that wisdom and experiential knowledge of God with her into the Nazi concentration camps and wherever she went throughout the rest of her life.

GODLY PEOPLE IN BUSINESS

If we want to have God in business, we need to have people who can *be godly* in business. We need to be people who demonstrate God's love, grace, and wisdom — whether we are an executive who leads, a welder who solders, a police officer who protects, a florist who arranges flowers, or an elected official who governs.

God's power is available to us in all that we do, the large and the small. Seek Him in the midst of your job and learn how to work with Him in His character and power. Let Jesus show you the way.

CHAPTER FIVE

NOT A TRIVIAL PURSUIT

Our purpose must then be to become one who loves others with Christ's agape. That purpose, when developed, will transform the social dimension of the human self and all of our relationships to others. Love is . . . the divine way of relating to others and oneself that moves through every dimension of our being and restructures our world for good.

DALLAS WILLARD

Perhaps you've heard the phrase, "The dead elephant in the middle of the room." It refers to the times when people ignore or sidestep the *real* problem. Everyone walks around the huge obstacle in the room, trying hard to ignore it. In business today, the dead elephant is ethics. Most metropolitan newspapers publish, on average, five hundred to a thousand articles every year dealing with the subject. Ethics in our classrooms, boardrooms, and offices is where the "light has gone out in our culture."[1] With all this attention, you would think we would have the problem licked, but we don't. Why?

I believe there are two reasons: the first is how we teach ethics and the second is how we think about ethics. The largest part of the problem is how our centers of knowledge deal with this. Our institutions of higher learning identify the fact that we have a problem, but they typically refuse to offer any guidance on how to be a good and ethical person. In his report for the academic year 1986–87, Derek Bok, former Harvard president, discussed the efforts of universities teaching ethics:

> Today's course on applied ethics does not seek to convey a set of moral truths but tries to encourage students to think carefully about complex moral issues. . . . . The principal aim of the course is not to impart "right answers" but to make students more perceptive in detecting ethical problems when they arise.[2]

In the conclusion of the report, Dr. Bok explains that institutions of higher education, and particularly the larger universities, do not treat ethics training as one of their responsibilities. This has changed to some degree since 1986, and virtually all universities have ethics classes, but they will admittedly only teach students how to think *about* ethics and would never presume to teach them *right from wrong* because they do "not seek to convey a set of moral truths." They believe that no moral truth exists (that wouldn't be tolerant or politically correct), so they only teach the process of identifying the factors to consider.

I'm personally aware of this failure. In 2005, my daughter took a college ethics class where she was taught to make ethical judgments based on the number of "happiness points" of one decision versus another. One part of the class examined the death penalty. (I wonder if the professor applied the same scoring system to that issue.) Right and wrong, good and evil were never discussed as truth, but as a relative point of view for determining the number of "happiness points." It's easy to understand why we are experiencing an ethical crisis in much of corporate America.

The other part of the problem is the lack of a clear understanding about the true meaning of ethics. The common understanding in business today is that ethics are needed so that we don't get in trouble or get sued, and if we do get in trouble, to show how hard we tried not to. That isn't ethics and doesn't always contribute to the common good.

VIRTUES: WINDOWS FOR GOD'S LIGHT

Ethics are based on, and sustained by, a desire to know and do what is good and right. The good and right thing includes avoiding or preventing what is evil and wrong. Knowing what is good and right is often referred to as morals. The duty to do what is good and right is ethics. Being ethical requires moral knowledge, being able to judge between good, better, and best, and choosing wisely a course of action based on the ultimate common good.

Our cultural inability to analyze carefully right and wrong, good and evil, especially in the university, has also stunted our ability to understand that determining what is good is *not* a simple topic. The offshoots of goodness can be found in words like *virtue, ethics, morals, love, service,* and *caring.* Unfortunately, Satan and our culture have eliminated many of these words from our vocabulary. Those that remain have been drained of their rich meaning, and what remains is often distorted. It's difficult to express how damaging it is to not be able to use the words we need to discuss this important subject. The words we need to publicly express ideas about goodness, godliness, holiness have been taken away or corrupted. So, however painful this might be, here is a quick course on Ethics 101.

The seven "classical" virtues are prudence, temperance, justice, fortitude, charity, hope, and faith.[3] C. S. Lewis groups the first four as cardinal virtues and the last three as theological. The cardinal virtues are those recognized by all civilized people as mandatory for society to function well and are called *cardinal* because the Latin root of *cardinal* means "hinge of a door" or "pivotal." A door doesn't work without the hinge, and society doesn't work without virtue. The theological virtues are those that stem from Christian sources.

Prudence is practical wisdom, the ability to think things through and come up with the course of action that is the best. This thoughtful, intentional, well-reasoned approach to living has at its core the knowledge of what good outcome is desired for the good of all that is in our care and how to arrive at that outcome.

Temperance is a well-measured and balanced approach to our actions. It keeps us from excess as well as deficiency. For those who indulge in too much TV, temperance is the decision to not watch any. For others, it is to watch only specific programs and only after more important matters are tended to.

Justice is righteousness, fairness, honesty, truthfulness . . . keeping promises along with honoring the law.

Fortitude is steadfastness in the face of danger and perseverance under pain or temptation.

Charity is to giving as poetry is to rhyming. If we believe that poetry is *just* rhyming words, we would be close to understanding what has happened to our idea about charity versus its original intent. Charity is Christian love, which explains why the older translations of 1 Corinthians 13 used the word *charity* where we now have *love*. When we love someone, we care for him and are willing to make sacrifices for him. We desire what is good for him and express our love in actions that promote what is good for him. Love is what propels us toward doing what is good, better, and best for people.

Hope is joyous anticipation of divine outcomes, a continual looking forward to the new world with Jesus on His throne, a peace and confidence in the good that God is doing here and now with us and through us.

Faith is confidence or trust—unwavering belief—in the reality of God and His kingdom. Faith is the substance of hope, the foundation that we stand on when we do what is good, right, and godly.

The virtues are characteristics of optimal goodness (goodness on steroids). They are indications of the depth of our character and our ability to act in love for someone (not just *feel* love for them). So love, service, caring, and goodness are intertwined. They are the root or foundation of a set of moral principles that weave the fabric of our life. *Character* is the word we use to describe someone's actions over time. When someone is of good character, it means that person has consistently displayed virtuous behavior over a sustained period of time and through various trials. We see that he or she has good moral and ethical character, and words like *noble* or *virtuous* are used to describe these individuals.

Ethics derives from the Greek word *ethos*, which the dictionary defines as "the disposition, character, or fundamental values of a particular person, people, or culture."[4] Seeking to know, understand, and apply moral knowledge to our self and our culture (ethos) is what we aim for in the study of ethics.

End of class.

STOP THE BLEEDING

Business is a large part of our nation's life, and the current state of ethics in the workplace penetrates deeply into every walk of life. Beyond formal ethical guidelines and codes of conduct, we also find ethics in a company's mission, vision, values, and goals statements. They are present in contracts, purchasing agreements, licensing, and warranties. Any document that states a company's character, behavior, or actions is a reflection of that company's morals and ethics.

The unwritten side to ethics is the actual behavior or culture (ethos) of a company, how the community behaves. Both are important, one as a statement of a company's ideals, vision, and dreams, the other as a gauge of how far they have to go to achieve the stated goal. One way that we are salt and light and good news to those around us is by guiding and influencing both the written vision and the cultural reality. Change in these areas takes patience, prayer, influence, and character.

There is a huge gap between today's ethics documents, which are mainly focused on litigation avoidance and public relations, and a meaningful ethics program. That's where God comes in. Read your company's current "ethics" document or "values statement" and ask the following questions: "Is this meant to keep me out of trouble or is it meant to help me be a better person, one of virtuous character? Is this meant to keep the company out of trouble or promote what is good and best within the company and its purpose for existing?" We have a responsibility to promote ethics programs that help bring God's plan for work into clear view and initiate healthy and productive community dialogue on topics of great importance. The place to start is by working through how to be a good person in your field of activity . . . and to clearly understand the good and right thing to do. Then pursue that course of action with God.

I have been blessed with many opportunities to provide wisdom and insight into this subject at work. One example came in a training class that was promoting a chaos theory approach to managing complex projects. The message to the students was that "change for change's sake" is how a company survives. It was a distorted form of survival of the fittest and how we must change or die. As part of the class assignment on promoting cultural change, I added the concepts of goodness, intrinsic human value, and humility, and I used the examples of John Wooden and the following quote by Antoine de Saint Exupery: "If you want to build a ship, don't drum up men to gather wood, divide the work, and give orders. Instead, teach them to yearn for the vast and endless sea."

Within each one of us is a yearning for something better, a desire to have our life and our work be meaningful and beneficial to others. And when I talk about this, people's hearts leap at the chance to discuss it. Everyone has within them a burning desire to have their work be valuable and meaningful. My presentation was the only one that received applause, generated lengthy conversation, and whose materials were requested by the instructor and class. When we decide to raise ethical awareness, we must have in our possession deep moral knowledge rooted in God, compassion for others, and the vocabulary needed to convey ideas like truth, godliness, virtue, nobility, righteousness, honor, justice, and character.

The usual lack of interest toward ethics programs is due largely to the fact that they contain nothing of importance or lasting value. Compare the ethics program of your company (or any random company found on the Internet) with the mission statement, oath, and law of the Boy Scouts of America.[5] I don't want to diminish the importance of people being well informed about the laws and regulations that affect the jobs they do, but that is legal compliance, not ethics, and the law is a starting point not an end point. Honoring the law is an ethical characteristic. Another common element of many ethics programs pertains to social issues such as diversity, tolerance, harassment (in all its forms), and financial integrity (these now fall under the heading of legal compliance). While these things are also important, their goals are just part of the natural outcome of an ethics program, not the core. You could satisfy all of these requirements and hardly rise above mediocre respectability. Keep in mind the words of C. S. Lewis: "Good and evil both increase at compound interest. That is why the little decisions you and I make every day are of such infinite importance."[6]

Most people in business sense this ethical gap but are challenged to express it because we don't have a cultural language of ethical principles and we are so afraid of offending people. I have enjoyed many wonderful conversations with two coworkers (one Buddhist and one Eastern Orthodox) about the purpose of work and the moral and ethical challenges our company and society face. We are able to discuss our religious and personal views on the subject of work and morals in a respectful and positive way, and we have developed a greater appreciation for one another.

Legal compliance and tolerance (as it is presently understood) are worthy goals, but they are not high ethical ideals. This is where God and the Bible come back into business, as guides and the best source of moral knowledge. *The focus of any ethics program should be the refinement of the heart and character of the individuals involved.* The goal should be to lead people forward in developing and maturing their character to the point where their actions can be judged to be righteous, virtuous, and noble. Compare this to being tolerant or keeping your company from being sued. Which effort has greater appeal to the unspoken desire of your heart?

IN THE TRADITION OF ABRAHAM

Legal compliance, tolerance, and financial integrity are all crucial and should be required, but we need to go beyond the "law" by working in the Spirit and with people to create and sustain loving work communities. The apostle Paul says, "But the fruit of the Spirit is love, joy, peace, patience, kindness, goodness, faithfulness, gentleness and self-control. Against such things there is no law" (Galatians 5:22-23).

One of the joys in doing research for this book has been finding individuals and communities who are shining examples of God's love in the world of business. It has been reassuring to see them doing good and going against the overwhelming trends of greed and inhumanity that seem to be so pervasive. The *Los Angeles Times* ran an article on such a person and boldly titled it "Being a CEO 'in the Tradition of Abraham.'" The article focused on Jonathan Swartz, the third-generation leader of the publicly owned Timberland company, and a meeting of the Jewish Federation that brought together seventy-five Jewish leaders from companies such as City National Bank, Cherokee, and Westfield to celebrate his godly example of business as God intended.

He was introduced as a "model of corporate and social responsibility," a member of President Bush's Task Force on National Service, and champion of his company's service program called the "Path of Service," which provides each employee of Timberland forty hours of paid leave to perform community service (paint a house, tutor a student, comfort the elderly). He summed up his beliefs by asking, "How do you maintain your values, even in the midst of day-to-day business dealings?" He answered by saying that the goal is to "integrate into daily life the value systems" that the Jewish tradition teaches. "In order to equip people to make their difference in the world, we must insist that doing well and doing good not be different." The article finishes with this quote from Mr. Swartz: "I haven't found a corporate environment where there aren't people who want to serve a truth greater than them."[7]

I work forty miles from my home and decided I wanted to minister to the disadvantaged kids in the area. I contacted a local church and signed up for a "helping children read" program. I have a coworker who is even more involved in benefiting other people. She is a member of the Latino Peace Officers Association, Hispanic Council, American Legion Auxiliary; she gives blood regularly, and plans on donating her hair for the second time to Locks of Love. Her nephew had leukemia and passed away four years ago, and she learned from that experience the need to be of service to others. She has said, "There is so much out there that people need. I feel blessed with a good job and good health—I want to serve those who aren't as fortunate."

Ethics is knowing *and* doing what is right and good. Faith is believing that God made us all with a desire to be noble and good, however dim and buried that spark might be. We must "fan into flame the gift of God" (2 Timothy 1:6).

WHAT DO YOU THINK ABOUT WORK?

Hundreds of books have been written on the subject of getting Sunday worship into weekday living. C. S. Lewis in *The Screwtape Letters* comments on the problem when he writes about modern man: "That might have been so if he had lived a few centuries earlier. At that time the humans still knew pretty well when a thing was proved and when it was not; and if it was proved they really believed it. They still connected thinking with doing and were prepared to alter their way of life as the result of a chain of reasoning."[8]

This is the gap between knowing and doing. We all risk living in conflict with our beliefs unless we intentionally set out to ensure that what we believe is rooted in confirmed personal experience (alter our way of life). It is through our personal experience that ideas become beliefs and become integrated in our living. Through our experience we come to know our beliefs are real. For clarity, I have chosen *ideas* and *beliefs* to denote the difference between a stated belief (idea), which only exists in our head and sometimes our mouth, and a confirmed belief (belief) that makes up the underlying knowledge and core-convictions that shape our actions and decisions.

We all believe in gravity and the chair that we are sitting in . . . until the chair breaks. Then our belief in gravity is confirmed, but our faith in chairs is put in doubt. Our confidence (faith) in God affects us in the same way. Do we trust Him? Is that trust rooted in confirmed personal experience or is He just a good-luck charm? Has something happened to erode our confidence? Do we rest in God's upholding and sustaining hand with the same confidence as the chair we're sitting in? Can we place the full weight of our life in God's hands and trust His promises?

TRUSTING HIM IN THE SMALL THINGS

The spiritual discipline of "small things" helps me learn how to live in God's promise to be with me always. Our lives are full of little things; even the big things that we do are made up of smaller, more modest tasks. There are three reasons why Jesus teaches us to submit the little things to God: (1) small things are easy to submit to God, (2) small things add up quickly to a day of doing God's will, and (3) the distraction of too many small things is one of Satan's most effective devices.

This discipline submits the little things to God by wrapping them in prayer. Picture the task and imagine placing it at the foot of the cross. Say the following prayer: "Dear Lord, I offer this up to you with thanksgiving and pray your blessing upon whomever it touches." (see Colossians 3:17). This might not be feasible for every task. Some jobs simply require very focused periods of sustained attention. I got the idea from the beautiful book *Introduction to the Devout Life*:

> [Regarding] ordinary affairs and occupations that do not require strict, earnest attention, you should look at God rather than at them. When they are of such importance as to require your whole attention to do them well, then too you should look from time to time at God, like mariners who to arrive at the port they are bound for look at the sky above them rather than down on the sea on which they sail. Thus God will work with you, in you, and for you, and after your labor consolation will follow. . . .
>
> Therefore, I earnestly counsel you to imitate the valiant woman whom the great Solomon praises so highly. As he says, she puts her hand to strong, generous, and exalted things, and yet does not disdain to spin and turn the spindle. "She has put her hand to strong things, and her fingers have taken hold of the spindle." Put your hand to strong things, by *training your-self in prayer and meditation*, receiving the sacraments, bringing souls to love God, infusing good inspirations into their hearts, and, in fine, by performing big, important works according to your vocation. But never forget your distaff or spindle. In other words, practice those little, humble virtues which grow like flowers at the foot of the cross: helping the poor, visiting the sick, and taking care of your family, with all the tasks that go with such things and with all that useful diligence which will not let you stand idle.
>
> Great opportunities to serve God rarely present them-selves, but little ones are frequent (emphasis added).[9]

God cares about everything in your life. He knows whenever a sparrow falls; He has counted the hairs on your head (easier for some than others); He has given names to each and every one of the stars; and He cares about us with a love that is beyond measure. So we must never question whether a thing is too small for God.

We can't give a day to God until we have first learned how to give single moments to God. In his book *A Game with Minutes*, Frank Laubach writes:

> We make Him our inseparable chum. We try to call Him to mind at least one second of each minute. We do not need to forget other things nor stop our work, but we invite Him to share everything we do or say or think. . . . While these two practices take all our time, yet they do not take it from any good enterprise. They take Christ into that enterprise and make it more resultful.[10]

Mr. Laubach teaches us to bring God into our thoughts on a frequent and regular basis in whatever way is helpful. In this way, he learned to keep God always before him. Jesus became such a comfortable presence in his life that he refers to him as his "chum." This is another way we can live a life where all the small things are done with and through Jesus; where "whatever you do, whether in word or deed," is as God would want.

How many times have we forgotten something important because we had too much on our mind? We suddenly realize that we have forgotten to pick up a present or send a letter or pay a bill because a thousand little things distracted us. This is why efforts to organize and to simplify are so popular and in most cases quite helpful because there are simply not enough hours in the day to get everything done that is being asked of us. Being organized is good, but knowing what *God* wants us to do is better.

PRACTICE· Find a way to bring the small things before the Lord. In the moment of deciding to do something, ask the Lord if it needs to be done. If you have decided that it does, then use one of the methods above to make it holy by bringing God into the doing. If it doesn't need to be done, then thank Him for the extra time and focus. Work toward having this become a habit by bringing Him into your mind frequently and regularly.

TEACHING THE WORLD TO READ

Frank Laubach had a deep personal experience with God and learned how to daily place the full weight of his life in God's hands. He had ups and downs as we all do, but he intended to live life fully with God. One day on top of a mountain, he beheld God and answered His call. He took up the cross that God gave him, and he dedicated the rest of his life to fulfilling that call. Frank Laubach believed that the world, in order to overcome hunger, disease, and oppression, needed to become literate, and this became his cross. Imagine taking on the effort to teach the whole world to read. His efforts created some of the most innovative and creative methods for teaching people how to read ever developed. In some cases, his methods realized results in one day. He saw these revolutionary methods translated into 315 languages, and countless millions owe their literacy to the tireless efforts begun by this man. In India from 1911 to 1931, there were five million new literate people counted in the census; from 1931 to 1951, thirty-six million new literate people were added. Ninety percent of those thirty-six million who learned in India used the method Laubach helped develop (more than a 600 percent increase!). When Frank Laubach gave his life fully to the Lord's work, nothing was the same for him or those touched by his work. His life was made new in discipleship to Jesus Christ and doing His Father's will. We can learn much from his example and the way he turned *everything* into something for God. Laubach wrote:

> Any hour of any day may be made perfect by merely choosing.
> It is perfect if one looks toward God that entire hour, waiting
> for his leadership all through the hour and trying hard to do
> every tiny thing exactly as God wishes it done, as perfectly as
> possible. No emotions are necessary. Just the doing of God's
> will perfectly makes the hour a perfect one. And the results
> of that one perfect hour, I believe, will echo down through
> eternity.[11]

CHAPTER SIX

TRAINING AS A DISCIPLE OF CHRIST

So as a disciple of Jesus, I have to know what are the things that will help me be His kind of person, where I am. And of course that means I'm a student of His. I study Him, I study what He says, but I have to go beyond that and learn the practices that will enable me to stay steady in His word, and in His life, and in my work. Because, you see, discipleship is not just a matter of learning what He says, but learning to do everything that I do in the way that He would do it if He were I.

DALLAS WILLARD

In Matthew 13, Jesus teaches a parable about a sower who threw seed on a field. Some of the seed landed where the soil was ready, some on rocks, some in the weeds, and some on the nearby path. To His disciples, Jesus explained that the seed was the Word of God and the places where it landed represents people's hearts. He goes on to describe that the conditions of the heart (soil) affect a person's ability to receive God's Word (the seed) in our life.

What part of our life is ready to receive the Word of God? When we think about our heart regarding work, is the soil soft and fertile, rocky, or weed infested? The "man who hears and understands" the message about the kingdom of God will produce a full harvest. But we shouldn't miss the aspect of the message that is for us to do: to make our heart ready to receive God's Word.

The culture of Jesus' day readily understood the relationship between the soil and the seed. They understood the work of the farmer in preparing the soil for planting and its impact on a crop. Adequately preparing the soil for planting didn't guarantee a bountiful crop, but lack of preparation ensured little or no harvest. We can't control the weather, and there's only so much we can do about bugs and weeds and drought, so those things we leave in God's capable hands. What we can do—what we must do—is prepare and tend the soil. We can do our part in being ready to receive God's living Word. Once planted, we watch and tend the crop, we remove the weeds, we water and we pray. With God at our side, we daily plant and tend and harvest the fruit of our heart.

I always had a passive impression of this parable until I read it as a farmer would. I assumed that once God's Word was in my heart, that was all there was to it. What I've learned is that my heart needs constant tending, and only God can help me. Spiritual disciplines help me come before the Lord so He can work on my heart. I have accepted responsibility for the spiritual condition of my heart and use spiritual disciplines to tend and cultivate His Word in my heart. Our heart is the center of our kingdom, and it is within the domain of our effective will. Our hearts must become the focus of our preparation and ongoing care, "for out of the overflow of the heart the mouth speaks" (Matthew 12:34).

OUT OF CONTROL

When I was young, my family used to watch *The Ed Sullivan Show*—and, yes, I'm old enough to remember seeing The Beatles on that show, but that's another story. Besides Topo Gigio (a little mouse puppet), my favorite act was the man who would balance plates by twirling them on top of tall, thin, flexible poles. He would start with a few plates, get them spinning really fast on their poles and then place them in holes in a long board on the floor in front of him. A fast spinning plate doesn't wobble, but a slow spinning plate does. He would add more and more spinning plates until some of the plates began to wobble. He would rush over and get them spinning again by grabbing the pole and whipping it around, then he would go back to adding more spinning plates. At some point, he would have so many plates spinning that there would always be multiple plates in various stages of wobble all up and down the row, right on the verge of crashing. He couldn't possibly keep them all spinning, and if he could, how was he going to get them all down without breaking any? I would yell into the TV, "Look out, look out, over there, get that one!" He was doomed.

It was an accident waiting to happen when there were more plates wobbling than spinning. Watching him run around, trying to keep all these plates in the air, was thrilling because there was no possible way, at least in my mind, of preventing the crash. He was running and sweating and dashing this way and that. In one last Herculean effort, he would rush down the line frantically getting the plates spinning again, and then one by one bring them down safely and take a bow. Little did I know how much that act would come to symbolize my life!

At one point in my life, I had so many plates in the air that most of them were wobbling and several were shattering on the ground. I couldn't keep up. I believed my work life was my real life, or at least the means to living a real life. There was a constant tension that existed between *real* life and work. I believed I needed to work long and hard to be successful—successful enough to begin "really living." I ended up working so hard that I lost whatever "life" I had. All the plates hit the ground and shattered while I stood in hopeless disbelief.

I worked very hard to be successful, and in the process I stopped living. The damage that I caused my family was immense, and the whole time I thought I was doing a great job because I was a good provider. I was lost. All the fulfillment, creativity, joy, and love that God desires for me was a thousand miles away. Running around trying to do it all on my own is no way to live. You've got to stop, give it all to Jesus, and learn how to truly live from Him. There is no comparison; there is nothing like Jesus.

In my industry, the joke is that working half days means only twelve hours a day. If you really get that joke or have told that joke, then you probably have too many wobbly plates. If you haven't learned how to say no to work, then you have too many wobbly plates. If you take work with you on vacation or answer your cell phone in the delivery room, then you have too many wobbly plates. It's a common problem, but *spinning is not the same as caring!* Our job is not a plate, our family isn't a plate, our soul is not a plate. They won't make do with snippets of our time. They are gifts from God. We must decide what is important, invest in those things, and say no to the rest. Without a clear understanding about the purpose of work, our job, and its place in our life, it will consume all that we have to offer and more. Work will not stop asking for more. William Law wrote:

> This is the only measure of our application to any worldly business, let it be what it will, where it will, it must have no more of our hands, our hearts, or our time than is consistent with a hearty, daily, careful preparation of ourselves for another life. For as all Christians, as such, have renounced this world to prepare themselves by daily devotion and universal holiness for an eternal state of quite another nature, they must look upon worldly employments as upon worldly wants and bodily infirmities, things not to be desired, but only to be endured and suffered till death and the resurrection has carried us to an eternal state of real happiness.[1]

Giving to work only what we should requires judgment, prayer, discernment, and arrangement. This can be one of the hardest things to accomplish, but without it work will have a tendency to consume more of your life than it should. In 2007, a season of change came into my life—for the first time in twenty years, I was working at home three days a week with a very flexible schedule. This shift coincided with a need at church because our senior pastor had resigned. All of a sudden, I was working side by side with the remaining pastors and preaching (something I had never done or been trained to do). As soon as our new senior pastor started, my flexible work schedule stopped. I don't believe that God would have been able to use me in this way if I hadn't been attentive to His will in my life.

Read James 4:17: "Anyone, then, who knows the good he ought to do and doesn't do it, sins." Now read Mark 9:30-31: "They left that place and passed through Galilee. Jesus did not want anyone to know where they were, because he was teaching his disciples." Jesus knew what he *ought* to do. There were plenty of people who needed healing and demons cast out and who were hungry, but that time was for teaching his disciples. We need to learn to say no so that we can say yes to what we ought to be doing.

Practicing spiritual disciplines helps us accomplish the "careful preparation of ourselves for another life." They provide us with opportunities to say no to the world and yes to God. This allows us to experience the grace of God by placing us in God's hand. They are part of our training program for reigning with Christ when He returns (see Matthew 25 and Luke 19).

WORKING BESIDE OUR FATHER

As a child I was blessed with the experience of working with my dad on projects around the house. I experience those same feelings when I am at work with God. I remember how special it made me feel to have my dad spend time with me and include me in things he was working on. He knew I would make mistakes, but he was always gentle and firm as he taught me how to do the task well. He would guide my hand until I could manage it on my own, and then he would give me more challenging tasks. I'm a father now and have the joy of teaching my children. We enjoy spending time together, and I love watching their faces beam with a sense of accomplishment as I praise their work. These times draw us closer, and it's why I love being a dad. I also know that I greatly influence how they will come to know their heavenly Father.

We've all been blessed with people who love us and who took time to teach us with their firm and patient instruction. They guided, supported, and instructed us, complimented us on our successes and pushed us to grow in our abilities. During these times more than knowledge is shared, more than wisdom is given. These times are bathed in love, and they have become a part of who we are. As a child we are drawn to the love of our father and mother and want to be accepted and guided by their love. As a parent we gain an understanding, however imperfect, of how much God desires to be with us and to teach us how to live and love and grow. When Jesus says that we must change and become like little children if we want to enter the kingdom of heaven, this is part of what He means. The joy and love that we felt as children is how our lives can be each moment with God. This is how it was meant to be. This is the good news about the kingdom of God: that Jesus is here to bring us to our Father so that He, through His Son and with His Holy Spirit, can teach us His ways.

As we grow and become more experienced, God will give us more to do: more challenging opportunities will be provided. In the midst of these challenges, we are never alone or left to struggle by ourselves. God is always watching us, loving us, and disciplining us so that we can grow into who He intended us to be. Jesus is there to make our burden light and has given us the Holy Spirit to guide and strengthen us.

HEARING GOD, STAYING STEADY

Learning takes humility. Humility comes from a heart of submission and gentleness and fear of God that softens our heart and opens our eyes and ears to learning His ways. As the apostle James wrote, "Who is wise and understanding among you? Let him show it by his good life, by deeds done in the humility that comes from wisdom" (3:13). Without humility we are a closed book, unable to learn.

Suppose there are two students. The first considers his teacher to be knowledgeable and wise and desires to learn what he has to teach. The second student thinks he knows it all. Which student will learn the most from the class?

Now imagine that there are two engineers. The first believes his creation is perfect and requires no improvements. The second engineer sees his creation as good and his best work, but understands that it can always be made better. Which engineer will learn and grow? Which design will be better able to accommodate future improvements?

Pride keeps us from learning and growing. Humility is *the* key to learning, which is why the Bible places such great emphasis on the necessity and blessings of humility and the damage of pride. You need humility to follow Jesus and learn from Him. The wisdom we are given then produces "humility that comes from wisdom."

DOES GOD SPEAK TO US?

Working with God, learning from Jesus, and gaining wisdom in His ways all require various forms of communication. In his book *Hearing God*, Dallas Willard points out four negative responses to the concept of God's communicating with us: (1) God would not communicate with run-of-the-mill human beings by surrounding them with His presence and speaking to them, (2) He does not communicate with us in that way, (3) God cannot speak to us, and (4) God shouldn't speak to us. Dallas answers that *God would* speak to us, *God does* speak to us, *God certainly can* speak to us, and *God should* speak to us.[2]

Hearing from God—actually communicating with God—makes a lot of people nervous. Jan Johnson talks about how many people think it is normal for us to pray to God, but crazy for us to hear something in return.[3] The most common question, and a really good one, is, "How do you know it's really God talking?" There are too many examples of people doing ungodly things "because God told them to." One helpful concept that comes from a number of Christian leaders is called the Three Lights. These lights are the Bible, our circumstances, and the Holy Spirit. I recently heard Rick Warren preach on this subject, and he added a fourth, "the godly wisdom of Christian counsel." By evaluating what we think God is saying to us within the context of these lights, we can be assured of its source and its rightness for our lives. What God says to us will always agree with the Bible, will harmonize with our present circumstances, and will be full of the Holy Spirit's power (and confirming with the godly Christians around you isn't a bad idea either).

Frederick B. Meyer's book *The Secret of Guidance* describes "circumstances, impressions of the Spirit, and passages from the Bible" as the basis of the Three Lights:

> God's impressions within and his word without are always corroborated by his providence around, and we should quietly wait until those three focus into one point. . . . If you do not know what you ought to do, stand still until you do. And when the time comes for action, circumstances, like glowworms, will sparkle along your path; and you will become so sure that you are right, when God's three witnesses concur, that you could not be surer though an angel beckoned you on.
>
> The circumstances of our daily life are to us an infallible indication of God's will, when they concur with the inward promptings of the spirit and with the Word of God. So long as they are stationary, wait. When you must act, they will open, and a way will be made through oceans and rivers, wastes and rocks.[4]

The apostle John tells us "Do not believe every spirit, but test the spirits to see whether they are from God" (1 John 4:1). And Paul admonishes us to "test everything. Hold on to the good" (1 Thessalonians 5:21). Therefore when we think we hear God speaking to us, we must test what we hear to determine if it is good and from God. The quality and nature, or character, of what is being said is one part of that testing, but the simplest test is if it is in harmony with the loving character of God. Does it conform to what Scripture tells us?

An examination of our conversation with God will never contradict the Bible (see 2 Timothy 3:16-17). God wants us to use Scripture to evaluate what we hear, the way the Bereans examined Paul's teachings: "Now the Bereans were of more noble character than the Thessalonians, for they received the message with great eagerness and examined the Scriptures every day to see if what Paul said was true" (Acts 17:11).

In *Hearing God* Dallas Willard considers John 10, where Jesus likens Himself to a shepherd and His followers to a flock: "When [the shepherd] has brought out all his own, he goes on ahead of them, and his sheep follow him because they know his voice. . . . My sheep listen to my voice; I know them, and they follow me" (verses 4,27). Dallas then goes on to write:

[These statements] are not merely a record of words that Jesus spoke. They are also an expression of John's own experience with Christ, his Lord and friend. . . . In the course of later experience John became so confident of the inner teacher that he could tell his children in the faith—even as he was warning them about those trying to deceive them—that they had no need of anyone other than the inner teacher, the Holy Spirit (1 John 2:27). . . . John therefore speaks to us from the authority of his experience, just as Abraham spoke to his eldest servant when sending him into an unknown land to find a wife for Isaac (Gen. 24) and just as Eli did to little Samuel (1 Sam. 3). We may mistakenly think that if God spoke to us we would automatically know who is speaking without having to learn, but that is simply a mistake—and one of the most harmful mistakes for those trying to hear God's voice. It leaves us totally at the mercy of any stray ideas we have picked up about what God's speaking is like.[5]

I'M LISTENING

The best example of hearing God that I can provide is my own. God said, "Spread My Word," and this book came from that experience. The words were simple, loving, and direct. They had, and continue to have, the most profound effect upon my life and those around me. I stood on a small hilltop and asked Him to speak to me, and He did. I understood that His Word was His living Word, the knowledge of Him and His presence in our world. When I came home and told my wife, she asked me "How?" (God bless the wisdom of a godly wife.) I told her that God hadn't provided the details, just the instruction. The details, as I would later learn, would be worked out in our continuing conversation. He has faithfully met my needs on this journey. The more I walked the path set before me, the more I needed and the more He supplied. Every time I tried to push it forward under my own power, the abundance would dry up, things would get much harder and go much slower. It is much easier, more fruitful, and a lot more fun (like riding a roller coaster blindfolded) to obediently follow Him.

One of the "details" that I was responsible for was how to interpret His request in my present circumstances. What did "Spread My Word" mean for me? I could have interpreted the message to mean that I would invest all that I had into printing and distributing Bibles or translating the Bible into other languages or bringing the gospel to people who couldn't read. My circumstances helped clarify my decision. They helped me see how to realize His will in my life, how my circumstances could be the means of doing His will. Work had been a great burden and challenge to me as a maturing disciple of Jesus Christ.

The absence of godliness in business was painful to me, and the lack of godliness from professing Christians at work weighed heavy on my heart. If they couldn't bring Christ into the workplace, what hope did I have? I quickly came to understand that my calling was to spread His Word within the realm of business, starting with my job.

Accepting His direction wasn't easy. I questioned my ability, my training, and my education. This took five seconds, and the answers were: none, none, and little or none. Everything you could imagine as a concern was asked and each one was answered by God. I knew I didn't know enough about God to spread His Word effectively, and I wondered who would listen if I tried. But through it all the Three Lights continued to guide me. The wisdom and counsel I found in *Hearing God* will be with me always.

> We must never forget that God's speaking to us, however we experience it in our initial encounter, is intended to develop into an intelligent, freely cooperative relationship between mature people who love each other with the richness of genuine agape love. We must therefore make it our primary goal not just to hear the voice of God but to be mature people in a loving relationship with him. Only in this way will we hear him rightly.[6]

I finally gave up my questioning and excuses and accepted His direction. As soon as I made that decision, the most amazing and exciting things began to happen. Opportunities opened up. Answers to my questions, wisdom about God's Word, resources that I needed were brought into my life. I had never taught a Bible study before, but was asked to lead one because of my passion about God in business. I have never written a book before, but I knew that my job was to do His will and let God be God regarding the outcome. This effort became, and continues to be, the guiding force and passion in my life. It has become my cross, and I willingly take it up each day. My lack of experience as a writer was a blessing because it humbled me and opened me to the wisdom of God, the Bible, and others. I had to surrender my limitations and weaknesses before God. I had to follow where He led, and it put me in a position of complete dependence upon His grace and blessing. His strength is made perfect in my weakness, and He has never let me down.

SILENCE BEFORE LISTENING

Since the world is a noisy place and our tongues are not easily tamed, silence should be observed as much as possible in the work environment. The helpful spiritual discipline of silence is intended to mature our ability to control the little beast in our mouth and train it in service to God (it also enhances the use of our ears). But before we teach it to fetch and roll over, we first need to teach it to sit. Being silent accomplishes three things immediately: (1) it gives us an opportunity to listen, (2) it gives God an opportunity to speak through others, and (3) it gives us an opportunity to think before we speak and to listen for what God wants us to say. I am not applying this discipline in the traditional method of staying silent for extended periods of time, although that can be beneficial; I mean pausing for a moment of silence to turn our ears to God and others. This isn't something that can be easily done in the middle of a heated conversation. This is something that must be practiced in calmer situations so that the "sit" command is well established when the heated conversation arrives.

The best way to start is *before* you speak. You may find it helpful to breathe before you speak, using the time during the breath to seek God's guidance. When people talk they usually want your attention and not necessarily your words, but it is human nature to offer little of the one and an abundance of the other. This discipline respects other members of the conversation and seeks to include God to the greatest extent possible. This discipline is equally effective for people who talk too much or too little, since it seeks to fill our mind and mouth with

God and reminds us to listen.

I love to talk. I used to think that all voids in any conversation were there for me to fill. So the result of this practice was profound. I was convinced my ideas needed to be heard, and I worked hard to make sure that they were and that I got credit for them. What I discovered in being silent was that others had similar ideas and by supporting their idea without seeking personal credit, I helped ensure acceptance of the idea (in other words, you've got to be okay with learning humility).

The experience was quite humbling. I discovered that when I was speaking for me, I wasn't really engaged in the conversation—I was just fighting to be acknowledged. I wasn't aware of God's presence, and I wasn't aware of others. The conversation was about people hearing what I had to say. Pride owned me. The discipline of silence taught me to listen, to be engaged, to respect God and others. I also learned that others would hear me better once they knew they were being heard. Over time this has significantly affected those tense conversations and helped me remain in His Word in the most difficult circumstances.

> **PRACTICE**• Before you speak, take a breath and seek God. Try practicing this with different types of relationships—friendly, contentious, professional, group.

WALKING ON OUR OWN

In 2 Chronicles 32, we read about Hezekiah, who was successful in everything he did, but on a certain occasion "God left him to test him and to know everything that was in his heart." We must anticipate and prepare for a time when we will have tribulations and God will seem far away. That is the point at which our virtue is tested and our heart is revealed. This is when God is like a parent letting go of a toddler learning to walk—He pulls His hand back just enough to let us walk on our own but remains close enough to catch us if we lose our balance or fall. He helps us get up until we can do so on our own; He steadies our steps until we can really walk on our own.

Oswald Chambers includes an excellent treatment of the process of developing faith in his book *My Utmost for His Highest*. He points out that many of us expect God to reward us for our faith, but there are times when God actually takes us off balance in order to help our faith grow. We may have had times of great joy and confidence in God, but "then God withdrew His conscious blessings in order to teach you to walk by faith. You are worth far more to Him now." It's easy and expected to "see God" when things are going well, but faith in God strengthens when He takes His hand away and still we believe and trust in His goodness and love.[7]

We are to be in the world but not of the world, being humble, fearing God, yearning to be in His presence, desiring to learn and grow in His wisdom and understanding. All these things are part of our small but necessary effort to grow in Christ, to allow God to make us more Christlike as each day comes. Frank Laubach approached it this way:

> As for me, I never lived, I was half dead, I was a rotting tree, until I reached the place where I wholly, with utter honesty, resolved and then re-resolved that I would find God's will, and I would do that will though every fiber in me said no, and I would win the battle in my thoughts. It was as though some deep artesian well had been struck in my soul. . . . You and I shall soon blow away from our bodies. Money, praise, poverty, opposition, these make no difference, for they will all alike be forgotten in a thousand years, but this spirit comes to a mind set upon continuous surrender, this spirit is timeless.[8]

Jesus calls us to be made complete in Him. In John 15:10-12, Jesus describes this process as His joy in us and our joy made complete. Our vision for this kind of life must be so wonderful and inspiring that we can't think of anything we'd rather be doing. If not, then the world will continue to entice and distract, and we will miss out on all that Jesus has promised for us. We must boldly step into the good that we intend because He is with His Father. As Elizabeth Rooney wrote in her poem "Opening":

> Now is the shining fabric of our day
> Torn open, flung apart, rent wide by love.
> Never again the tight, enclosing sky,
> The blue bowl or the star-illumined tent.
> We are laid open to infinity,
> For Easter love has burst His tomb and ours.
> Now nothing shelters us from God's desire—
> Not flesh, not sky, not stars, not even sin.
> Now glory waits so He can enter in.
> Now does the dance begin.[9]

When we commit ourselves to truly becoming disciples of Christ, everything about our lives is revolutionized. Our burdens are lifted, and we are empowered by the Spirit to live fully for Him. The dance begins.

CHAPTER SEVEN

THE NUCLEUS OF CHANGE

*Fortunate or blessed are those who are able to find or are given a path
of life that will form their spirit and inner world in a way that is truly
strong and good and directed Godward.*

DALLAS WILLARD

The word *life* covers a lot of ground—who we are, what we do, what we've done, who we are becoming. It is helpful to look at smaller pieces in order to think about it more clearly. Our life consists of who we are as a person—heart, soul, mind, strength, and relationships (see Mark 12:30-31). It also consists of what we do—job, ministry, work. There was a time in my life when I didn't understand the importance of honoring all the parts of my life beyond my job. I didn't know how important they were. I also didn't fully appreciate the impact of who I was on those around me and how I affected them. I had no real sense of who I was becoming. Like Scrooge, I was unaware of the chain I was forging. A great deal of what I have learned comes from this simple diagram and what it represents:

THE CIRCLES OF OUR LIFE

God never intended our jobs to push the rest of our lives out of balance. No job can bear the weight of a person's whole life or be the only place where his character is formed. Look at the diagram above; each circle represents an element of living (job, ministry, and work), and each has a proper place within the broader context of our life. Our job represents what we do for a living, what we get compensation for (money or something else). Our ministry/calling is that part of God's specific plan He has given us to accomplish in our lifetime. Work encompasses the total amount of lasting good you will accomplish. Think of this in terms of the complete works of Shakespeare or Leonardo da Vinci. Now multiply that for each "circle" to get a lifetime of "work." For most of us, this circle is filled with our loving service to family, friends, and neighbors. Life represents the whole package of who you are.[1]

So who we are (heart, soul, mind, strength, relationships) is present and active in what we do (job, calling, work, life). A full life means that no circle gets so large for so long that it crowds out the others, and each circle is filled with Christ's love flowing through us. The third dimension of the diagram represents how each part of our living rests upon and "grows" out of the one below. Our life springs forth from God; our work springs forth from our life; our ministry springs forth from our work; our job springs forth from our ministry. For any circle of our life to be a foundation for the others, our whole life must rest upon the rock that is Jesus Christ, and we must bring Jesus into each part.

LIVING UPSIDE-DOWN

God is most interested in the person you are becoming—the life circle. Once we decide to give our life to God, then we bring His name and love fully into who we are. Our relationship with God is the strong foundation that supports our life. Trying to have our job be the foundation for our life (flipping the pyramid upside-down) is the greatest threat confronting individuals and our culture today. No matter what your occupation, your job can't read a bedtime story to your child, kiss your spouse, coach Little League for you, or care for your elderly parents. For many people (including me for many years), our job is our idol. A life lived upside-down will eventually tip over and shatter. How many times have we seen and heard about that happening? Someone loses his job or has trouble at work, and the rest of his life is put on hold or, in the all-too-often extreme, he goes on a killing rampage or commits suicide.

When we give our life to God, He begins a process of transformation. We follow Jesus and learn how to live. As we do that more and more, every circle of our life, every part of who we are, is increasingly filled with the light of God's abundant love. God loves us and wants us to build a personal relationship with Him, to live our lives in His kingdom through His Son and be filled with His Spirit. To achieve that kind of life requires more than saying it is so; it requires humbly opening our heart in the confident assurance it is so. Inviting God into every aspect and element of our life is the only way that we can bring Him into the workplace. It is through us that God wants to have His will done in all the areas of our life, including our job.

FROM THE GROUND UP

Having secured our life on the foundation of Jesus Christ (the life circle), we can then bring God's love into the work circle, which includes our relationships with family, friends, and neighbors. We learn to love them as Jesus does, and our love is expressed in action. These acts of loving service become our treasure in heaven. And these acts of service to family, friends, and neighbors naturally move us into the ministry circle.

Our unique talents, coupled with God's purpose, move us in the direction of our effective ministry. It is from the strength and goodness of this circle of loving relationships and acts that we can step out into the broader community with love and have a heart rich toward God and others. Families teach us how to be of loving service toward others; they teach us kindness and forgiveness; they guide us in the ways we should live and help us see how God has uniquely shaped us. We must ensure that we can be of loving service to our families before we attempt to minister to those outside of our family. Rooted in the strength of our life in God and family, our ministry/calling can be sustained, infused, and strengthened by God.

With the other foundational circles firmly in place, God brings us to the job circle. Fully rooted in God and His kingdom, we are prepared to blossom in other ways. His abundance will flow into the work that we do, and we will be the channel for His love into that place and time. The job can change, it can be taken away or be incredibly challenging, but it doesn't have the ability to shake the rest of our life because our life is firmly built and rests secure in Jesus.

Rooted in and *resting upon* are terms I use to convey two parts of living. Part one is the sense of having something firm to stand upon and spring forward from. We can feel secure in the action that we are taking. And part two is the sense of being nourished, sustained, rooted, and strengthened by something that never runs dry. We have confidence in the power and provision that we need for the things we ought to be doing.

Not everyone "grows" into the circles in this way. Many of us come to Jesus later in life, having already followed whatever path we chose to our present job. Similarly, people can have significant change take place in their lives and might need to start over. These circles are to help you look at your life and think about it in a new and helpful way. No one has a "perfect" alignment.

LIFE IS LIKE A DONUT?

No diagram can adequately portray a life. No life can be represented by a bunch of circles or a pie or a donut. Even if we agree with the abstract groupings, they don't convey the interconnectedness of each part with the others. They can only be tools to help us think about our life. Certainly, the lines of separation between job and ministry can be blurred, such as if your job is being a pastor. The lines between job and family can blur if you are in a family business or working with family members. And parents who stay home to care for children don't think there are any lines between work, ministry, and job . . . life *is* caring for children.

For most of us, our job constitutes 50 to 70 percent of our waking hours! The goal is to set your rule of life (God should get the first fruits of your time) and find a balance point or range of hours that defines the acceptable boundaries for your job and the other elements of your life. There is no hard and fast eight-hour rule for your job, but at the end of a week if you've not spent any meaningful time with God, family, friends, or ministry, then you need to adjust your boundaries.[2] Try to maintain your boundaries and honor your limits, but be sensible enough to understand that life will always keep tension on them and you need some flexibility and guidance from the Holy Spirit. With this "balance point" in place as a guide, your job can be a positive and nurturing part of your life. With your job in its proper place in your life, the blessing of work as a loving place of mutual benefit and support can flow into who you are becoming and what you are doing.

Here's an example: Let's say you work for a company located in a community that is in need of medical services for the poor. You see the need and decide to address it. This decision affects your actions—what you do during your lunch break, committees you join, churches and charities you contact, prayers you offer, what you talk about with family, friends, and coworkers. You might elicit help from your employer to set up and support a local clinic where you can volunteer. So your job and ministry would converge or overlap. As a result of this involvement, your company becomes more aware and involved in the local community, and the involvement might begin to extend to other community services and other communities. None of this can happen if you spend too much time at work.

We are God's means of connecting people so that needs can be known and met. Our job is more than just exchanging our time for money. The local need could be schools, daycare, parks, the environment, or any number of things. The point is to open up our vision of "job" to see the broader fabric of life that touches all God's children.

Think of your work, ministry, and job as areas of your life where you can bear fruit through word and deed. Think of the Holy Spirit as the life-giving sap that runs through us and into the fruit that we bear. Think about Jesus as the way to bind our life to God as a branch is grafted to a tree. By placing our life in God's hands, by being the branch that is attached to the vine, our life draws upon the abundance of God and we produce much good fruit (see John 15).

GOD AS THE NUCLEUS OF WORK

Jesus told us, "Let your light shine before men, that they may see your good deeds and praise your Father in heaven" (Matthew 5:16). What would happen if we consciously sought to apply this passage at work every moment of every day? Would we perform our jobs differently? How would our relationships with vendors, stockholders, coworkers, and customers change? What impact would we have upon the individual lives of the people involved? How would we treat the local community and the environment? Moses laid down his staff, the primary tool of his profession, and took it up again for the Lord. In some ways he remained a shepherd, but in other ways his work was profoundly changed. The same is true for us. As a police officer, fire fighter, banker, or waitress, how would you "lay down your staff" before God? I have come to understand that there aren't secular jobs, only secular people. A priest or pastor can be just as secular as a plumber or lawyer if he hasn't decided to give his work over to the Lord. William Law wrote:

> As a good Christian should consider every place as holy because God is there, so he should look upon every part of his life as a matter of holiness because it is to be offered unto God. The profession of a clergyman is a holy profession because it is a ministration in holy things, an attendance at the altar. But worldly business is to be made holy unto the Lord by being done as a service to Him in conformity to His divine will.[3]

Our decision to follow Jesus might not change anything that people can see (title, compensation, employer). The dramatic change occurs wherever we make room for God to be actively present in our work. When He is present in the heart, mind, soul, strength, and relationships of a follower of Jesus Christ, everything changes.

INFLUENCE AND IMPACT

I once heard a sermon that illustrates the ripple effect of our actions, or what I refer to as the circles of influence and impact. The underlying theme was that we never know what effect our actions might have, but that each one of us is able to dramatically impact the world for good or evil. In this sermon, the preacher told of Mikhail Gorbachev, then leader of the Soviet Union, who ultimately dismantled the most powerful communist country in the world, the USSR. Gorbachev was asked, "Who is your role model?" He identified Lech Walesa, the first freely elected prime minister of Poland and a man who spent a great deal of time in prison in his quest for human rights as leader of the Labor Movement. When asked the same question, Lech Walesa said, "Martin Luther King Jr.," whose nonviolent protests for civil rights changed the face of America. Martin Luther King Jr.'s role model was Rosa Parks for her strength in refusing to give up her seat on a bus. That action led to the bus strike in Mobile, Alabama, that began what we know as the Civil Rights Movement in America. Rosa Parks recently passed, and her body lay in state in our nation's capital, where tens of thousands of people came to pay their respects.

Rosa Parks influenced Martin Luther King Jr., who, in turn, influenced Lech Walesa, who then influenced Mikhail Gorbachev. The ripple of Rosa Parks' saying no could be seen as influencing the end of the Cold War, the fall of the Berlin Wall, the reunification of Germany, the fall of the USSR, and the movement of democracy into communist countries in Europe that were dominated by communism for over fifty years. Rosa accomplished it by saying no when it needed to be said and by being willing to go to jail for what was right. Our actions can ring far and wide. We never know where they will stop or how God might empower them. We need to do the right thing and let the sound of God's truth ring loud in the world. The circles of influence and impact follow this ripple effect. Being salt and light to the world is the Christian term for having influence and impact on those around us.

The concept of circles of influence and impact takes this basic idea and applies it to the workplace and the formal and informal authority we have there. Let's define some terms: *Authority* is a degree of power, or sway, over individuals and decisions. There are two types of authority in the workplace, formal and informal (I sometimes use the term *influential*).

Formal authority is assigned to an individual and agreed to by the leaders of a business. It is usually paired with title—president, vice president, director, manager, supervisor—and some form of job description that defines the scope of authority and responsibility. Other examples are accountants, auditors, quality assurance inspectors, and so on, because they all carry some degree of formal authority. Formal authority will always have a defined *circle of impact*—the people and things that will be affected by their decisions.

Informal authority or influence is predominantly derived from experience, character, and relationship. Everyone has some degree of both types of authority as a part of his or her job. When Rosa Parks said no, she was operating with influential or informal authority, and what she ran into was formal authority, the bus driver and the police. Mother Teresa and Martin Luther King Jr. are good examples of the effectiveness of informal authority and how the circle of influence concept works.

I have learned to ask two questions when I need to get something done at work: Who's responsible? and Who can make it happen? The name is usually different for each question. Where I work, there is a man named Roger who is a simple computer programmer, yet he holds a position of great informal authority. No changes can be made to an entire suite of applications without him saying it is okay. Major projects have been funded based on his advice. Roger isn't on any boards, doesn't hold any significant title, and there is virtually no documentation identifying him as the single point of authority. But he is. Meetings with VPs will be rescheduled if he can't attend. After years of hard work, dedication, and demonstrating an amazing ability to memorize thousands of lines of code, he is the acknowledged expert. At my previous job, it was Jay. He, too, had little *formal* authority but lots of *informal* authority.

Other terms for influence are credibility, trust, experience, and reputation, which all convey the idea of being able to affect how people think about things. Informal authority flows or influences along various lines of communication and relationship, and these form the circles of influence. The circles of influence are more subtle than circles of impact in how they operate, but they are typically more powerful because they are based on trust, culture, and relationship.

AUTHORITY VERSUS TRUTH

When people with formal authority ignore truth and the reality of God and His kingdom, their decisions typically find opposition from those who value truth. This tension is found in Ephesians 6, where we are called to obey our earthly masters and a few verses later called to struggle against the rulers, powers, and authorities of this dark world. How do we know when the line has been crossed and we are called to resist, instead of obey, authority? When should we struggle (use our authority) and say no and set ourselves against the powers of this dark world? I don't know a single person in the workplace today who has not been confronted with this dilemma.

There are three keys to discerning our course of action in these situations: (1) knowing the nature and purpose of work as God intended, (2) our intimate conversational relationship with God (remember the Three Lights), and (3) the regular practice of spiritual disciplines (see the section Practice Taking Responsibility in chapter 3). Combined, these help us to remain strong and give us the wisdom to discern the difference between the requests that we should obey and those we should resist. They help us to know the actions to take, and they strengthen us to be able to do what's right regardless of the consequence. It is often enough that we don't participate in worldly activities, like rumors or harsh criticism, but there will be times when action is called for. It is times like these when reputation and influence can matter most.

As we continue our walk with Jesus, we will increasingly find ourselves making more godly decisions and taking more godly actions. Sometimes more risk is involved, but that provides more space for God. Our life will be filled with God when we do what's right and rest in the assurance of God's character and power. God did not save Shadrach, Meshach, and Abednego from being thrown into the fire, but He protected them in the midst of it.

Let me be candid on this point. If you take actions to resist evil that go against formal authority, you will be at risk, and you will probably experience hardship. But the Lord will always strengthen those whose hearts are fully committed to Him (see 2 Chronicles 16:9). Having done what is right, you will grow in your trust and personal experience of God. Along the way you could lose your job, you could be demoted, or you could be ridiculed by friends and coworkers who might criticize you and distance themselves from you. I have experienced most of these things, but during these same periods of struggle I have felt completely at peace in God's strength and surrounded by His love. I have been richly blessed with the abundance and faithfulness of God. I would rather suffer loss with God at my side then triumph without Him.

THAT HE MAY BE GLORIFIED

Our job is a way for us to glorify and honor God and be a blessing to others. Honoring God by honoring our "masters" means performing our jobs in such a way that God is honored, glorified, and given thanks through His Son Jesus Christ in the simple act of our daily work. William Law compares the job of the clergyman with the tradesman to demonstrate the grace and holiness available in all occupations:

> Let him but intend to please God in all his actions as the happiest and best thing in the world, and then he will know that

there is nothing noble in a clergyman but a burning zeal for the salvation of souls, nor anything poor in his profession but idleness and a worldly spirit.

Again, let a tradesman but have this intention and it will make him a saint in his shop; his everyday business will be a course of wise and reasonable actions made holy to God by being done in obedience to His will and pleasure.[4]

We live and rest in the assurance that God is in charge, that nothing is impossible for Him. Jesus had no money, He had no official "power base," He had no marketing department or formal authority from the world. His disciples have been described as a motley crew at best, made up of a few fishermen, a tax collector, and others. The moral police of the day, Pharisees, had nothing good to say about Jesus or the people He associated with. Yet Jesus and His followers were able to change the world. Jesus tells us that we will do even greater things than He did because He is with His Father in heaven. Who are we to doubt Him? Who are we to question our role and purpose in doing God's will?

Doing my job within God's kingdom is the most exciting and challenging experience that I know. It is all at once peaceful and powerful, loving and courageous, gentle and strong. There is no life for me outside His love — no color, no joy, no heart. I come before Him in childlike awe and reverence, and He takes my hand and guides me to places that I have never been. I'm doing things with Him I never dreamed I would ever do. He asks me to do things I've never done before and don't feel capable of, but when I follow His lead, all that I need is provided. I see people around me changed and affected by His loving hand. I see my life following a path I had never seen and didn't even know existed. Through all my failings, fears, stumbles, frustration, and worry, I feel His understanding and love, His words of comfort and mighty strength. When He draws His hand away, I know that He stands not far off, watching for my feeble steps and smiling at my progress and forgiving me in my failure.

Work *is* a fundamental structure of love in the kingdom of God. It is a loving structure that sustains, creates, endures, and supplies all we need in abundance. I come to work in loving community with God's children, to develop and invest my talents for the mutual benefit of those I work with and those who are blessed by what we do. And while I contribute my skills, I benefit from the contributions of others who provide me with what I need. The desk I work at, the clothes I wear, the electricity and water, the computer, the building, and so much more are provided by God to accomplish the tasks He's called me to perform. I strive for perfection in my chosen field of endeavor and help others to see the great importance of the work they do and the value they have as children of God in meeting the needs of others. What more could I ask for?

THE END AND THE BEGINNING

This book ends in hope—a prayerful hope that it has given you a new way to think about work and ways to put those thoughts into action. It is a joyful hope that many more will come to know what God intended and find ways to make room for Him in their work. It is a passionate hope that we can pass on to our children a brighter reflection of the beauty and blessing of work. It is an assured hope in the power of Jesus Christ to be with us always and teach us everything we need to follow Him into the abundant, eternal, and full life of His Father's kingdom. Let us join together in making this our prayer and our promise:

And whatever you do, whether in word or deed, do it all in the name of the Lord Jesus, giving thanks to God the Father through him.
COLOSSIANS 3:17

HOW GOD IS IN BUSINESS[1]

DALLAS WILLARD

My objective is to change people's minds. I gave up a long time ago trying to get people to do things and decided instead to help them think things through and come to a different view of matters. I knew that would change their feelings and would lead them to doing different things. My main goal is to help them come to a correct understanding of who they are and where they are, and then they, together with the Lord, can begin to participate in the right kinds of activities.

With this in mind, I want to address the topic, "How God Is in Business." I'm going to use the term *business* rather generously. It will cover everyone who is here and fundamentally the broader context of professional life that most of us exist in. But I want to speak in such a way that it covers all of us and the things we're doing to make a living and, beyond that, to serve our community.

Let me start with a passage from the apostle Paul, that great teacher and leader for Christ: "Slaves, in all things obey those who are your masters" (Colossians 3:22, NASB). Many people today will say, "Well, that's me!" But these were real slaves, and it certainly applies to all of us today who try to serve others by working. Paul goes on to say that slaves should obey their masters "not with external service, . . . but with sincerity of heart, fearing the Lord. Whatever you do, do your work heartily, as for the Lord rather than for men, knowing that from the Lord you will receive the reward of the inheritance" (verses 22-24, NASB). Note the simple starkness of the last sentence: "It is the Lord Christ whom you serve" (verse 24, NASB).

This is a radical change in the understanding of what work is, what a job is, and what business is, and it can only be understood in the context of the kingdom of God. I'm not going to try to exhort you to get God into business; I'm just going to try to explain to you two main ways that He *is* in business, and we have to come to terms with it because He is there.

The first way is simply this: Business is God's arrangement. Human beings didn't think it up. They put some variations on it, but it is a part of God's design, by which human beings love and serve one another. It is an extension of the basic human relationships that we have in family, which reach out to neighbors and communities, and it is a fundamental structure of love in the kingdom of God. I'll say that again: Business is a fundamental structure of love in the kingdom of God.[2]

That's where we have to start. We read in the psalms and other Scriptures how God looks down from heaven and observes the hearts of human beings. I especially like 2 Chronicles 16:9: "The eyes of the LORD move to and fro throughout the earth that He may strongly support those whose heart is completely His" (NASB). That's a basic picture that we must never forget. God is on the job, business is His business, humanity is not a human project. Humanity is God's project, and He is bringing out of it an amazing community of redeemed souls, which He will dwell in for eternity. We each get to be a part of that.

One of the things I often point out in teaching about the kingdom of God is that our role in our present life is *training for reigning*. That applies to business. Often, when we look at business and the fine details, especially the religious business, it doesn't look like God is in control. That's because He has made space for us to learn to live under Him and to love our neighbor as ourselves, while we are at the same time loving Him with all our heart, soul, mind, and strength. As a result, there's much professional tension today, in all of the professions. The old professions are, of course, the clergy, law, and medicine. My work provides me with opportunities to talk to a lot of doctors' and lawyers' groups. It's unfortunate, but I think I can make a general statement today that nearly all in those professions feel like the conditions under which they practice their work militate against the very purpose for which they went into their work in the first place.[3]

I meet a lot of ministers who testify to that same sort of thing. They're just beaten to death by the things that are pushed upon them in their job. I meet a lot of mothers who feel that way about it too. We move in a world that, it seems, constantly harasses us and distracts us from the purposes that in our heart of hearts we feel we should be fulfilling.

We need to talk a moment about why that is. It really is because the standards of success that are accepted and that people are held to in the various lines of work confuse us about what we're really supposed to be doing. It's often said in church-growth circles that the ABCs of success in the church are "attendance," "buildings," and "cash." We understand where that's coming from because we can easily draw that conclusion by just standing on the sidelines and watching who gets applauded and rewarded.

Some time back it struck me that, when I was young, we didn't ask if our ministers were successful. Just to check my memory, I asked my wife, Jane, "Did we think of ministers in terms of success or not?" She confirmed to me that we really didn't think in those terms. We believed that they had a call in their lives and they were doing the best they could to fulfill that call. And we knew that sometimes they failed and that some were more entertaining to listen to. Of course, there were many ministers who were not good speakers and others who were not well educated, yet they were faithful men who, over the years, did a tremendous work for God. But if we try to judge them by the ABCs, they flunk.

I watch my students go off to law school, all full of ideas. They're going to serve justice, and their hearts are aflame with it. They come back in two years pretty well squashed. And then, perhaps two years after that, I see them, and they have come to understand that the system of law they're involved in does not have an awful lot to do with justice.

I spoke to a group of doctors from Hollywood Presbyterian Hospital some years back, and nearly every one of them was arranging to retire. They were searching for a way to get out of the business and save themselves physically and financially. This is a tough thing. On the one hand we want to say, "So how is God in business?" Well, God is in business because He's in everything, and business is His arrangement. We need to respect that and know that, but on the other hand, when we look at the fine structure, we see there's a real problem. We need to spend some time talking about why that is so.

We live in a period of great moral confusion. When we think about serving others, for example, we need to ask, "What does that mean?" When we think about loving others, loving our neighbor, what does that mean? In western culture today, there are two broad responses to love or service. Hardly anyone rejects love or service outright; they're seen as good things. And in business people emphasize the importance of service, but what does it mean?

Today when we talk about loving someone, it often means that we must be prepared to approve of what they desire and the decisions that they make, and to help them fulfill those goals. So in effect we are told, "If you love me, you will do what I want you to do." Now that gives a whole new meaning to service. And that can even lead us, in the church situation, toward simply trying to do what people want in order to get them to come back.

The same principle is true at a business or in an educational institution. At the University of Southern California, where I teach, we have no meaningful undergraduate requirement in mathematics for the whole degree program. I venture that's true in more universities than you might suppose. And the reason is because the students don't want it. That raises an issue: Perhaps there's another meaning to love and service that we need to think about.

Here's a second meaning: To love and serve people means to favor what is good for them, and to be prepared to help them fulfill it, even if that means disapproving of their desires and decisions, and attempting to, as appropriate, prevent their fulfillment. The fact that someone wants something doesn't necessarily mean it's in his best interest, does it?

Let me go over these two meanings again, because this is fundamental to the whole idea of serving others. One way of thinking about service is, "I love you, and I'll serve you by doing what you *want* me to do." That's perhaps one of the most common ideas today. The other idea is, "I love you, and I will serve you by doing what is *good* for you, whether you want it or not." You see the difference? Now, you might say to a young person, "You need to know mathematics whether you want to or not." It's a little late when they get to the university to do that, but that's another story.

Still, the difference here is what is good for you and what you want. The issue is whether or not you can think in terms of serving people just by giving them what they want. And the answer is: You can't. You cannot do that. And in order to stand on this principle, you need a point of reference beyond what people want. That's where God comes back into business.

God gives us a point of reference for determining what is good for people independently of what they want. That's why it's so important in the family to have this point of reference, but it's equally important in the schools, and it's equally important in business. If you look at it historically, if you look at the literature regarding business, you will see that *the aim of business is to make provision for the needs of the people in an area.* That's the aim of business. In older days it was largely physical needs, but today of course, in the age of information, it's going to involve intellectual or mechanical or technical needs—all kinds of needs to be met. Still, the basic aim of business is to make provision for the needs of the people in an area served.

Notice the way this is developing. If a business actually does make that provision, it is successful. Well, immediately the response comes back, "But does it make a lot of money?" Here I'm going to say something that will strike many people as heretical: The aim of business is not to make money. Just like the aim of churches is not to attract people. Is it important to make money? Yes, it is. Is it important to attract people to church? Yes, it is. But that's not the mark of success. And that's where we have to have a different place to stand.

I say to you very simply that the only place we can stand is in the teachings of Jesus Christ. He is the only one who can give us the guidance we need in order to serve others, whatever our line of work may be, and wherever we are in that line of work. We have to be able to stand there.

This brings us to the subject of discipleship. I want to apply it particularly to the area of work. *The place of discipleship is wherever I am now. It's wherever I am now, and whatever I am doing now.* If we don't understand that, then most of our life will be left out of the place of discipleship. It may be home, work, play, or church, but discipleship should take place wherever I am now.

When I go to work at USC and I walk into a class, that's my place of discipleship. That's the place where I am learning from Jesus how to do everything in the kingdom of God. I am constantly learning it, and I am a long way from the end of the lesson. Sometimes I'd just as soon the lessons stop, but they don't because life moves on and students are different and colleagues change. The areas of thought that I write about and work in change, so I have to be reconciled to the fact that I am going to be a disciple of Jesus from here on.

That's why it's important for me to understand that Jesus is, in fact, the smartest man in my field. He's the smartest man in your field. It doesn't matter what you're doing. If you're running a bank or a mercantile company or a manufacturing plant or a government office or whatever it is, He's the smartest man on that job.

So we're constantly in school under Jesus' authority and tutelage. He is our master and teacher. That's the teaching that Paul gives us in Colossians: "Whatever you do, whether in word or deed, do it all in the name [that is on behalf of and in the power] of the Lord Jesus, giving thanks to God the Father through him" (3:17).

I'm not just giving a religious lesson—I'm talking about life. I'm saying that if we are going to accept God in business, we need the kind of people who can be godly in business. I remember Al McDonald, the head of Jimmy Carter's White House staff, once came to a seminar I gave. After my presentation, he came up to me and asked, "How do you get Christianity into the boardroom?" My answer was very simple: "Have a Christian walk in and sit down." There isn't any other way.

That's the other part of the answer to the question, "How is God in business?" He is in business because the business is His, because the world is His. Not only the cattle but the Cadillacs on a thousand hills belong to Him, and the BMWs, too. It all belongs to Him. But He has left a space where we have to make the choice to be His people in the midst of His world. And we have to overcome these dreadful moral confusions that rest upon our world. They prevent us from understanding that serving really involves giving people what is good for them, not merely pursuing their approval and granting their desires. I hope you see the difference between these, because this is the breakpoint upon which our culture is standing at present.[4]

What is it to be a good person in business? We have a lot of courses now in business ethics and professional ethics that are not about ethics at all. Courses in professional ethics and texts in professional ethics are basically studies in how to stay out of trouble—and that's not a high moral ideal. The emphasis is on how to stay out of trouble with your clients, your fellow professionals, and the law. If you read those texts and go to conferences on these subjects, you'll see that they don't touch the basic issue in professional ethics, which is how to be a good person through your field of activity. Understanding how to be a good person—that's where the light has gone out in our culture. It comes as a real shock to many young people to realize that you could be successful and not be a good person. That's because they now are given no way of thinking about what it is to be a good person.

A morally good person is someone intent upon advancing the various goods of human life with which they are in effective contact. This individual does this in a manner that respects the relative degrees of importance and the extent to which the actions of the person in question can actually promote the existence and maintenance of those goods—the various goods of human life. Being a good person yourself is among the most important of those goods. So to promote moral goodness in yourself and others is a very important part of being a good person. Elton Trueblood somewhere echoes the voice of an older moralist that the only really good thing is a good person.

Our confusions now are so deep on these matters that most people cannot say exactly what it means to be a good person and then put that idea into the context of their work. Young people especially have trouble here. I find older people have had enough experience to know they've got to do something about being good, and they usually have worked their way through to some sensible version of it. Of course Christian folks normally feel like there's a great obligation on their part to bring Christ into work and make Him a substantial part of who they are as a teacher, a banker, a lawyer, and so forth.

Who is a good person? From the Christian point of view, a good person is one who loves God with all his heart, soul, mind, and strength, and loves his neighbor as himself (see Luke 10:27). And then we need to add that among Christians the ideal is a little higher. That is, we should love one another *as* Christ has loved us.

So love is the center of goodness. It's the driving force in all our activities. When I walk into my classes, if I don't love those students, I have failed. But suppose they believe I only love them if I give them what they want. Doing so would be to betray them, wouldn't it? So I must have an understanding of goodness that allows me to get beyond their wants and desires. I must stand as a whole and strong person who carries through with a consistent line of activity that will really help them, because if I only do what they want, it will ultimately harm them.

To accomplish this, I must take care of myself. I cannot just let myself go — I must train myself as a disciple of Jesus Christ. I have to learn how to be a whole person. I have to make sure I don't make the mistake of thinking that I can, for example, just work hard and be successful. I reiterate this point because it's one of the major problems of our day: People believe that if they work hard enough, they'll become successful, and that's the chief aim in life.

A couple of weeks ago, I heard a man teach at the University of Beijing, and he talked about what has happened to young people in China and how they define success. It is simply money, money, and more money. They go to the universities, and their object is to do the best they can in their courses, get the best possible positions, so they can make the most possible money. And that is as far as they go. We've got a lot of people in the U.S., too, many times in our churches, who really don't view success as anything beyond that. They do not understand what it means to be a whole person, living under God, with other people who are going through life on their way to eternity. That is a lost concept to them.

So as a disciple of Jesus, I have to know what kinds of things will help me be His kind of person, where I am. A significant part of this means I'm a student of His. I study Him, I study what He says, but I have to go beyond that and learn the practices that will enable me to stay steady in His Word, and in His life, and in my work. Because discipleship is not just a matter of learning what He says, but learning to do everything I do in the way that He would do it if He were I.

So I have to have a pattern of discipline in my life that enables me to steadily feed and nourish my soul and my body with the things that will enable me to be God's person where I am. I'm not talking about being the local Christian nag. I'm talking about being the kind of person in whom God shines so brightly that people wonder what's going on. You remember Jesus' words, "Let your light shine before men in such a way that they may see your good works, and glorify your Father who is in heaven" (Matthew 5:16, NASB).

You want a kind of light and power living in you that is so great that people never make the mistake of thinking it comes from you. Jesus said that "a city set on a hill cannot be hidden" (Matthew 5:14, NASB). We don't have to nag. We don't have to be sure that we get in our negative points. Very often it's sufficient to stand up for righteousness by simply remaining in cheerful noncompliance with evil. Simply don't participate. When we're expected to lie, we don't lie. When we're expected to gossip, we don't gossip. When we're expected to hurt other people who have hurt us, we don't do that. That's just a part of what comes from this light of Christ in us.

We should also expect that there will be evidence of a supernatural hand of God in the work we do. That's a part of discipleship too. A part of discipleship is learning how to fulfill our responsibilities and complete our tasks in such a way that God will be manifestly present in that work.

William James once said, "Keep the faculty of effort alive in you by a little gratuitous exercise every day. That is, be systematically heroic in little unnecessary points." I like that language. He also said:

> Every day do something for no other reason than its difficulty, so that when the hour of dire need draws nigh, it may find you not unnerved and untrained to stand the test. Asceticism in this sort of thing is like the insurance which a man pays on his house and goods. The tax does him no good at the time, and possibly may never bring him a return, but if fire does come, his having paid it, it will be his salvation from ruin. So with the man who has daily inured himself to habits of

concentrated attention, energetic volition, and self-denial in unnecessary things. He will stand like a tower when everything rocks around him, and his softer fellow mortals are winnowed like chaff in the blast.[5]

Now, that's a merely human approach. Add to it, "Take your cross and follow Christ." Now you step out of the merely human. You can't disregard the merely human, but you need to put on top of it the grace of God and discipleship to Christ that involves self-denial practiced in a regular way, both for the benefit of the quality of your work and the quality of your relationships; and as you do that, then you begin to see the fruit of a life that is lived fully in the kingdom of God.

Take a look at this diagram. Think about your job, your ministry, your work, and your life. It is extremely important for you to distinguish those things if you're going to take care of yourself and be the kind of person who can stand in the world of business as a whole person for Christ.[6]

Let me just briefly describe them. Your job is what you get paid to do. You can immediately see that for many people there's a problem in that their job will become their whole life. That's a threat that hangs over us.

Then there's your ministry, which is that part of God's work He has entrusted to you. There are some things that God specifically wants done in your time and in your place, and He's given those things to you to do. It may be a lot of different things. If our task is as pastor or teacher or something of that sort, then ministry may be a bigger part of our life. But even so, our job and our ministry are two different things.

Your work is the total amount of good that you will accomplish in your lifetime. For many of us, our family will be a large part of that. I say that because in being Christ's person in the world today, we need to make sure that we don't sacrifice our family to our ministry or to our job.

Encompassing all of this is your life. That's you. God is more interested in your life than He is in any of the other things there. He's more interested in the person you are becoming than in your work or your ministry or your job. If you are careful to distinguish between *who you are* and *what you do*, then you'll have a basis to stand in the face of the pressures that can tear you apart in this world. And you will be a whole person, and your family will be whole, and you'll do wonderful work, and you will bring God into your work wherever you may be, because you've allowed God to live in you completely. If you don't, God will still bless you in some measure. You'll still go to heaven when you die, if you trust Jesus, but your life may be rather sad.

What follows is a touching poem that helps us see the pathos of a life in which we have not received God fully:

The wind, one brilliant day, called to my soul,
　　with an odor of jasmine—
and the wind said, in return for the odor of my jasmine
　　I'd like all the odor of your roses.
But I said I have no roses—

All the flowers of my garden are dead.
And then the wind said, well I'll take the withered petals
 And the yellow leaves.
 And the wind left.
 And I wept.
 And I said to myself:
"What have you done with the garden
 that was entrusted to you?"[7]

To each of us is given a garden. It is our life. God gives us all the grace and wisdom we will need if we will cultivate it under Him. And when we do, wherever we are in life, God will be there.

Author's note: *The following papers (Riskin, appendix B, and Brandeis, appendix C) are included, challenging language and all, because they articulate what isn't being spoken of today — the responsibility and value of the professions toward enhancing public life and the common good. Trust for the professions today is all but gone, and their contribution to society often questioned. Within our society the basic understanding that the professions were to contribute to the common good and not their own advancement is a distant memory. So we must look back and see where we've come from to chart a path forward and re-instill into the professions the heart of goodness that allowed them to serve the public well.*

UNTO THIS LAST

JOHN RUSKIN[1]

The fact is, that people never have had clearly explained to them the true functions of a Merchant with respect to other people. I should like the reader to be very clear about this.

Five great intellectual professions, relating to daily necessities of life, have hitherto existed — three exist necessarily, in every civilized nation:

The Soldier's profession is to *defend* it.
The Pastor's, to *teach* it.
The Physician's, to *keep it in health*.
The Lawyer's, to *enforce justice* in it.
The Merchant's, to *provide* for it.
And the duty of all these men is, on due occasion, to *die* for it.

"On due occasion," namely:

The Soldier, rather than leave his post in battle.
The Physician, rather than leave his post in plague.
The Pastor, rather than teach falsehood.

The Lawyer, rather than countenance injustice.

The Merchant—What is *his* "due occasion" of death?

It is the main question for the Merchant, as for all of us. For, truly, the man who does not know when to die, does not know how to live. Observe the Merchant's function (or manufacturer's, for in the broad sense in which it is here used the word must be understood to include both) is to provide for the nation. It is no more his function to get profit for himself out of that provision than it is a clergyman's function to get his stipend. The stipend is a due and necessary adjunct, but not the object, of his life, if he be a true clergyman, any more than his fee (or *honorarium*) is the object of life to a true physician. Neither is his fee the object of life to a true merchant. All three, if true men, have a work to be done irrespective of fee—to be done even at any cost, or for quite the contrary of fee; the Pastor's function being to teach, the Physician's to heal, and the Merchant's, as I have said, to provide. That is to say, he has to understand to the very root the qualities of the thing he deals in, and the means of obtaining or producing it; and he has to apply all his sagacity and energy to the producing or obtaining it in perfect state, and distributing it at the cheapest possible price where it is most needed.

And because the production or obtaining of any commodity involves necessarily the agency of many lives and hands, the Merchant becomes in the course of his business the master and governor of large masses of men in a more direct, though less confessed way, than a military officer or Pastor; so that on him falls, in great part, the responsibility for the kind of life they lead: and it becomes his duty, not only to be always considering how to produce what he sells in the purest and cheapest forms, but how to make the various employments involved in the production, or transference of it, most beneficial to the men employed.

And as into these two functions, requiring for their right exercise the highest intelligence, as well as patience, kindness, and tact, the

Merchant is bound, as Soldier or Physician is bound, to give up, if need be, his life, in such way as it may be demanded of him. Two main points he has in his providing function to maintain: first, his engagements (faithfulness to engagements being the real root of all possibilities in commerce); and, second, the perfection and purity of the thing provided; so that, rather than fail in any engagement, or consent to any deterioration, adulteration, or unjust and exorbitant price of that which he provides, he is bound to meet fearlessly any form of distress, poverty, or labor, which may, through maintenance of these points, come upon him.

Again: in his office as governor of the men employed by him, the Merchant or manufacturer is invested with a distinctly paternal authority and responsibility. In most cases, a youth entering a commercial establishment is withdrawn altogether from home influence; his master must become his father, else he has, for practical and constant help, no father at hand: in all cases the master's authority together with the general tone and atmosphere of his business, and the character of the men with whom the youth is compelled in the course of it to associate, have more immediate and pressing weight than the home influence, and will usually neutralize it either for good or evil; so that the only means which the master has of doing justice to the men employed by him is to ask himself sternly whether he is dealing with such subordinate as he would with his own son, if compelled by circumstances to take such a position.

Supposing the captain of a frigate saw it right, or were by any chance obliged, to place his own son in the position of a common sailor; as he would then treat his son, he is bound always to treat every one of the men under him. So, also, supposing the master of a manufactory saw it right, or were by any chance obliged, to place his own son in the position of an ordinary workman; as he would then treat his son, he is bound always to treat every one of his men. This is the only effective, true, or practical Rule that can be given on this point of political economy.

And as the captain of a ship is bound to be the last man to leave his ship in case of wreck, and to share his last crust with sailors in case of famine, so the manufacturer, in any commercial crisis or distress, is bound to take the suffering of it with his men, and even to take more of it for himself than he allows his men to feel; as a father would in a famine, shipwreck, or battle, sacrifice himself for his son.

All which sounds very strange: the only real strangeness in the matter being, nevertheless, that it should so sound. For all this is true, and that not partially nor theoretically, but everlastingly and practically: all other doctrine than this respecting matters political being false in premises, absurd in deduction, and impossible in practice, consistently with any progressive state of national life; all the life which we now possess as a nation showing itself in the resolute denial and scorn, by a few strong minds and faithful hearts, of the economic principles taught to our multitudes, which principles, so far as accepted, lead straight to national destruction. Respecting the modes and forms of destruction to which they lead, and, on the other hand, respecting the farther practical working of true polity, I hope to reason further in a following paper.

BUSINESS: A PROFESSION

LOUIS D. BRANDEIS[1]

The peculiar characteristics of a profession as distinguished from other occupations, I take to be these:

First. A profession is an occupation for which the necessary preliminary training is intellectual in character, involving knowledge and to some extent learning, as distinguished from mere skill.

Second. It is an occupation that is pursued largely for others and not merely for one's self.

Third. It is an occupation in which the amount of financial return is not the accepted measure of success.

Is not each of these characteristics found today in business worthily pursued?

The field of knowledge requisite to the more successful conduct of business has been greatly widened by the application to industry not only of chemical, mechanical, and electrical science, but also the new science of management; by the increasing difficulties involved in adjusting the relations of labor to capital; by the necessary intertwining of social with industrial problems; by the ever extending scope of state and federal regulation of business. Indeed, mere size and territorial expansion have compelled the business man to enter upon new and broader fields of knowledge in order to match his achievements with his opportunities.

This new development is tending to make business an applied science. Through this development, the relative value in business of the trading instinct and of mere shrewdness have, as compared with other faculties, largely diminished. The conception of trade itself has changed. The old idea of a good bargain was a transaction in which one man got the better of another. The new idea of a good contract is a transaction that is good for both parties to it.

Under these new conditions, success in business must mean something very different from mere money-making. In business the able man ordinarily earns a larger income than one less able. So does the able man in the recognized professions — in law, medicine or engineering; and even in those professions more remote from money-making, like the ministry, teaching or social work. The world's demand for efficiency is so great and the supply so small, that the price of efficiency is high in every field of human activity.

The recognized professions, however, definitely reject the size of the financial return as the measure of success. They select as their test, excellence of performance in the broadest sense — and include, among other things, advance in the particular occupation and service to the community. These are the basis of all worthy reputation in the recognized professions. In them a large income is the ordinary incident of success; but he who exaggerates the value of the incident is apt to fail of real success.

To the business of today, a similar test must be applied. True, in business the earning of profit is something more than an incident of success. It is an essential condition of success; because the continued absence of profit itself spells failure. But while loss spells failure, large profits do not connote success. Success must be sought in business also in excellence of performance; and in business, excellence of performance manifests itself, among other things, in the advancing of methods and processes; in the improvement of products; in more perfect organization, eliminating friction as well as waste; in bettering the condition of the workingmen, developing their faculties and promoting their happiness; and in the establishment of right relation with customers and with the community.

In the field of modern business, so rich in opportunity for the exercise of man's finest and most varied mental faculties and moral qualities, mere money-making cannot be regarded as the legitimate end. Neither can mere growth in bulk or power be admitted as a worthy ambition. Nor can a man nobly mindful of his serious responsibilities to society, view business as a game; since with the conduct of business human happiness or misery is inextricably interwoven.

Real success in business is to be found in achievements comparable rather with those of the artist or the scientist, of the inventor or the statesman. And the joys sought in the profession of business must be like their joys and not the mere vulgar satisfaction which is experienced in the acquisition of money, in the exercise of power or in the frivolous pleasure of mere winning.

It was such real success, comparable with the scientist's, the inventor's, the statesman's, which marked the career of William H. McElwain of Boston, who died in 1908 at the age of forty-one. He had been in business on his own account but thirteen years. Starting without means, he left a fortune, all of which had been earned in the competitive business of shoe manufacturing, without the aid of either patent or trademark. That shows McElwain did not lack the money-making faculty. His company's sales grew from $75,957 in 1895 to $8,691,274 in 1908. He became thus one of the largest shoe manufacturers in the world. That shows he did not lack either ambition or organizing ability. The working capital required for this rapidly growing business was obtained by him without surrendering to outside investors or to bankers any share in the profits of business: all the stock in his company being owned either by himself or his active associates. That shows he did not lack financial skill.

But this money-making faculty, organizing ability, and financial skill were with him servants, not masters. He worked for nobler ends than mere accumulation or lust of power. In those thirteen years McElwain made so many advances in the methods and practices of the long-established and prosperous branch of industry in which he was engaged, that he may be said to have revolutionized shoe manufacturing. He found it a trade; he left it an applied science.

This is the kind of thing he did: in 1902 the irregularity in the employment of the shoe worker was brought to his attention. He became greatly impressed with its economic waste, with the misery to the worker and the demoralization which attended it. Irregularity of employment is the worst and most extended of industrial evils. Even in fairly prosperous times the workingmen of America are subjected to enforced idleness and loss of earnings, on the average, probably ten to twenty percent of their working time. The irregularity of employment was no greater in the McElwain factories than in the other shoe factories. The condition was not so bad in shoe manufacturing as in many other branches of industry. But it was bad enough; for shoe manufacturing was a seasonal industry. Most manufacturers closed their factories twice a year. Some manufacturers had two additional slack periods.

This irregularity had been accepted by the trade—by manufacturers and workingmen alike—as inevitable. It had been bowed to as if it were a law of nature—a cross to be borne with resignation. But with McElwain an evil recognized was a condition to be remedied; and he set his great mind to solving the problem of irregularity of employment in his own factories; just as Wilbur Wright applied his mind to the aeroplane, as Bell, his mind to the telephone, and as Edison, his mind to the problems of electric light. Within a few years irregularity of employment had ceased in the McElwain factories; and before his death every one of his many thousand employees could find work three hundred and five days in the year.

Closely allied with the establishment of regularity of employment was the advance made by McElwain in introducing punctual delivery of goods manufactured by his company. Shoes are manufactured mainly upon orders; and the orders are taken on samples submitted. The samples are made nearly a year before the goods are sold to the consumer. Samples for the shoes which will be bought in the spring and summer of 1913 were made in the early summer of 1912. The solicitation of orders on these samples began in the late summer. The manufacture of the shoes commences in November; and the order is filled before July.

Dates of delivery are fixed, of course, when orders are taken; but the dates fixed had not been taken very seriously by the manufacturers; and the trade was greatly annoyed by irregularities in delivery. McElwain recognized the business waste and inconvenience attendant upon such unfulfilled promises. He insisted that an agreement to deliver on a certain day was as binding as an agreement to pay a note on a certain day.

He knew that to make punctual delivery possible, careful study and changes in the methods of manufacture and of distribution were necessary. He made the study; he introduced the radical changes found necessary; and he so perfected his organization that customers could rely absolutely upon delivery on the day fixed. Scientific management practically eliminated the recurring obstacles of the unexpected. To attain this result business invention of a high order was of course necessary — invention directed to the departments both of production and of distribution.

The career of the Filenes of Boston [founders of Filene's department stores] affords another example of success in professionalized business. In 1891 the Filenes occupied two tiny retail stores in Boston. The floor space of each was only twenty feet square. One was a glove stand, the other a women's specialty store. Twenty years later their sales were nearly $5,000,000 a year. In September, 1912, they moved into a new building with more than nine acres of floor space. But the significant thing about their success is not their growth in size or in profits. The trade offers many other examples of similar growth. The pre-eminence of the Filenes lies in the advance which has been made in the nature, the aims and ideals of retailing, due to their courage, initiative, persistence and fine spirit. They have applied minds of a high order and a fine ethical sense to the prosaic and seemingly uninterested business of selling women's garments. Instead of remaining petty tradesmen, they have become, in every sense of the word, great merchants.

The Filenes recognized that the function of retail distribution should be undertaken as a social service, equal in dignity and responsibility to the function of production; and that it should be studied with equal intensity in order that the service may be performed with high efficiency, with great economy and with nothing more than a fair profit to the retailer. They recognized that to serve their own customers properly, the relations of the retailer to the producer must be fairly and scientifically adjusted; and, among other things, that it was the concern of the retailer to know whether the goods which he sold were manufactured under conditions which were fair to the workers — fair as to wages, hours of work and sanitary conditions.

But the Filenes recognized particularly their obligations to their own employees. They found as the common and accepted conditions in large retail stores, that the employees had no voice as to the conditions or rules under which they were to work; that the employees had no appeal from policies prescribed by the management; and that in the main they were paid the lowest rate of wages possible under competitive conditions.

In order to insure a more just arrangement for those working in their establishment, the Filenes provided three devices:

First. A system of self-government for employees, administered by the store co-operative association. Working through this association, the employees have the right to appeal from and to veto policies laid down by the management. They may adjust the conditions under which employees are to work, and, in effect, prescribe conditions for themselves.

Second. A system of arbitration, through the operation of which individual employees can call for an adjustment of differences that may exist between themselves and the management as to the permanence of employment, wages, promotion or conditions of work.

Third. A minimum wage scale, which provides that no woman or girl shall work in their store at a wage less than eight dollars a week, no matter what her age may be or what grade of position she may fill.

The Filenes have thus accepted and applied the principles of industrial democracy and of social justice. But they have done more — they have demonstrated that the introduction of industrial democracy and of social justice is at least consistent with marked financial success. They assert that the greater efficiency of their employees shows industrial democracy and social justice to be money-makers. The so-called "practical business man," the narrow money-maker without either vision or ideals, who hurled against the Filenes, as against McElwain, the silly charge of being "theorists," has been answered even on his own low plane of material success.

McElwain and the Filenes are of course exceptional men; but there are in America today many with like perception and like spirit. The paths broken by such pioneers will become the peopled highways. Their exceptional methods will become accepted methods. Then the term "Big business" will lose its sinister meaning, and will take on a new significance. "Big business" will then mean business big not in bulk or power, but great in service and grand in manner. "Big business" will mean professionalized business, as distinguished from the occupation of petty trafficking or mere money-making. And as the profession of business develops, the great industrial and social problems expressed in the present social unrest will one by one find solution.

NOTES

FOREWORD

1. Phillips Brooks, *Best Methods of Promoting Spiritual Life*
(New York: Thomas Whittaker 2&3 Bible House), 12–13, 35.

PROLOGUE

1. David Willman, "Hidden Risks, Lethal Truths," *Los Angeles Times*, June 30, 2002. The article begins "Newly obtained internal documents show that Warner-Lambert Co. executives who promoted the diabetes pill Rezulin masked from federal regulators early indications of the drug's danger to the liver and later delayed sharing information about its lethal toxicity with family doctors." The article documents the impact to patients: "The FDA now attributes 94 liver failures, 66 of them fatal, to Rezulin." Another article on that same day by the same writer, titled "Strategy Developed to Get Latinos to 'Take the Risk,'" describes how Warner-Lambert targeted Latinos. The article quotes a Warner-Lambert memo dated March 31, 1998: "It is clear that in the Miami area, a more aggressive approach to promoting Rezulin needs to be undertaken in the Hispanic community."

2. Enron's behavior is so well known that no reference is required, but an article from David Streitfeld and Lee Romney, run in the *Los Angeles Times*, January 27, 2002, titled "Enron's Run Tripped by Arrogance, Greed" will help clarify the point I'm making. WorldCom, Arthur Anderson, Tyco International, Adelphia Communications, Rite Aid, Global Crossing, KPMG, HomeStore, and ImClone were all part of the moral failure of businesses between 2000 and 2002. A search on any major metropolitan newspaper for that period is overwhelming. Citigroup, JPMorgan Chase, Merrill Lynch, and Charles Schwab were in the backdrop of the accounting scandal (see *CNNMoney*, January 20, 2003). Catholic Healthcare West (*Los Angeles Times* June 8, 2002). Kaiser's kidney transplant program failures (*Los Angeles Times* July 26, 2007).

3. Matthew 14:13: "When Jesus heard what had happened, he withdrew by boat privately to a solitary place." Matthew 14:23: "After he had dismissed them, he went up on a mountainside by himself to pray. When evening came, he was there alone." Mark 1:35: "Very early in the morning, while it was still dark, Jesus got up, left the house and went off to a solitary place, where he prayed."

4. Richard Foster, *Celebration of Discipline* (New York: Harper and Row, 1978), 1.

5. Douglas J. Rumford, *SoulShaping* (Wheaton: IL: Tyndale, 1996). Also see the website: http://instructor.prairie.edu/StevenIbbotson/CMFX105/class3.htm.

6. John Ortberg, "Rethinking the Kingdom of God: The Work of Dallas Willard and Some Applications to Psychotherapeutic Practice," *Journal of Psychology and Christianity*, vol. 14, no. 4, 1995.

CHAPTER 1

1. Studs Terkel, *Working: People Talk About What They Do All Day and How They Feel About What They Do* (New York: New Press,

1972), xi. This book, more than any other, articulated for me the existing conditions of work as most of us experience it. It gives voice to the workers and helped me to see how desperate the need was to address those conditions and how much we need Jesus at work.

2. The two Hebrew words here are *abad* and *shamar*. *Abad* is translated as *work*, *cultivate*, or *tend*. *Shamar* is translated as *take care of*, *keep*, *care*, or *care for*. Although I use *care* as the operative translation, I also enjoy the *keep* translation because it also means to treasure or protect.

3. Nancy Henderson Wurst, "Doing the Right Thing," *Spirit*, May 2003. This article was also published in NADS (National Association for Down Syndrome), http://www.nads.org/pages_new/human_interest/doingtherightthing.html.

4. Lee Hardy, *The Fabric of This World* (Grand Rapids, MI: Eerdmans, 1990), 85.

CHAPTER 2

1. For a more in-depth discussion about God's kingdom, I suggest reading chapter 3 of *The Divine Conspiracy* (New York: HarperCollins, 1998) by Dallas Willard.

2. For the best understanding about the spiritual disciplines, please read *Celebration of Discipline* (New York: HarperCollins, 1978) by Richard Foster and *The Spirit of the Disciplines* (New York: HarperCollins, 1988) by Dallas Willard.

3. C. S. Lewis, *Mere Christianity* (New York: MacMillan, 1952), 150.

4. There are multiple references to the spiritual formation concept. I highly recommend *Renovation of the Heart* (Colorado Springs, CO: NavPress, 2002) by Dallas Willard as the best book about spiritual formation and to help gain a fuller understanding about the various aspects of self that are involved in kingdom living.

5. Dallas Willard, *Renovation of the Heart* (Colorado Springs, CO: NavPress, 2002), 197.

6. Richard Foster, *Celebration of Discipline* (New York: Harper and Row, 1978), 97.

7. Frank C. Laubach, *Man of Prayer* (Syracuse, NY: New Readers Press, 1990), 74–75. From The Heritage Collection of Selected Writings of a World Missionary. This book is one of the best on prayer, journaling, and the effect of God on those who seek Him.

8. William Law, *A Serious Call to a Devout and Holy Life* (New York: Paulist Press, 1978), 236.

9. Lewis, *Mere Christianity*, 153.

10. Henri Nouwen, "Moving from Solitude to Community to Ministry," *Leadership* magazine, Spring 1995.

11. Dallas Willard, *The Divine Conspiracy* (New York: HarperCollins, 1997), 271.

CHAPTER 3

1. Monopolies and Cartels—corporations and groups whose aim is to establish a monopoly or to control a market through devious means for purposes of power and greed. Some of the practices employed are: dumping—used in international trade to bank-rupt foreign markets; predatory pricing—similar to dumping but is market based; price discrimination and price fixing—the act of varying prices to achieve, promote or sustain a monopoly; zone pricing—intended to cover certain variable costs but can be misused to achieve, promote, or sustain a monopoly. Examples: British East India, U.S. Steel, AT&T, OPEC, Archer Daniels Midland Company. Read Connor, John M.—The Food and Agricultural Cartels of the 1990s. Department of Agricultural Economics, Purdue University, 2002.

2. Carl von Clausewitz, *On War* (New York: Oxford University Press, 2007), 13.

3. John Helyar, "Sweet Surrender," *Fortune*, October 14, 2002.

4. Dr. John Patrick gave a talk entitled "What Hippocrates Knew and We Have Forgotten," which highlights the ordinal position of truth over loyalty in a Judeo-Christian culture and the reverse in a pagan society. He points out the caustic and destructive qualities of societies that held loyalty over truth and gives Nazi Germany as an example. C. S. Lewis says something similar in *Mere Christianity* when talking about the virtues: "There is not one of them which will not make us into devils if we set it up as an absolute guide" (C. S. Lewis, *Mere Christianity* [New York: Macmillan, 1952], 10).

5. Richard Lacayo and Amanda Ripley, "The Whistleblowers," *Time*, December 30, 2002/January 6, 2003.

6. Dallas Willard, *Renovation of the Heart* (Colorado Springs, CO: NavPress, 2002), 131.

7. Lewis, *Mere Christianity*, 22.

8. Lee Hardy, *The Fabric of This World* (Grand Rapids, MI: Eerdmans, 1990), 69.

9. Mother Teresa, Nobel Lecture, December 11, 1979, http://nobel-prize.org/nobel_prizes/peace/laureates/1979/teresa-lecture.html.

CHAPTER 4

1. C. S. Lewis, *Mere Christianity* "The Three Parts of Morality" (New York: Macmillan, 1952), 57–58.

2. This phrase is well used by Dallas Willard when he helps people see who they truly are. C. S. Lewis wrote an essay titled "The Weight of Glory," and I recommend it to you for more elaboration on this subject.

3. Christian Legal Society is an organization dedicated to "doing justice with the love of God." Write On is in the entertainment industry and works with screenwriters to bring knowledge of God into entertainment. St. Thomas University School of Law works specifically to produce Christian lawyers dedicated to serving Christ in their field of endeavor. ServiceMaster is a publicly

traded company whose four key objectives are: To honor God in all we do; To help people develop; To pursue excellence; To grow profitably. There are so many more that it was a difficult challenge to pick just a few.

4. John Wooden, "Cooperation," The Pyramid of Success, The Official Site of John Wooden, http://www.coachjohnwooden.com/.

5. Lee Hardy, *The Fabric of This World* (Grand Rapids, MI: Eerdmans, 1990), 48.

6. Jan Johnson, *When the Soul Listens* quoted in foreword by Dallas Willard (Colorado Springs, CO: NavPress, 1999), 7.

7. Dallas Willard uses this phrase, or one very much like it, when he teaches on spiritual disciplines and fasting. In his book *The Spirit of the Disciplines*, he wrote "Fasting confirms our utter dependence upon God by finding in him a source of sustenance beyond food" (Dallas Willard, *The Spirit of the Disciplines* [New York: HarperCollins, 1988], 166).

8. Jeremy Taylor, "The Benefits of Fasting," *The Whole Works of the Right Rev. Jeremy Taylor*, (London: Henry G. Bohn, 1851), 477.

9. Frank C. Laubach, *Man of Prayer* (Syracuse, NY: New Readers Press, 1990), 238.

10. Corrie ten Boom, *In My Father's House* (New York: Hodder & Stoughton Religious, 1976), 167.

CHAPTER 5

1. See Dallas Willard's message "God in Business," in appendix A of this book.

2. Derek Bok, "The President's Report 1986–87" (Cambridge, MA: Harvard University Press, 1987), 2–3.

3. I was unable to find a definitive and agreed-upon list of virtues. Another "classic" list is courage, truth, honor, fidelity, discipline, hospitality, industry, self-reliance, and perseverance. Either one will do for purposes of our discussion.

4. *The American Heritage Dictionary of the English Language*, fourth ed. (Boston: Houghton Mifflin Company, 2000).

5. Mission statement: "The mission of the Boy Scouts of America is to prepare young people to make ethical and moral choices over their lifetimes by instilling in them the values of the Scout Oath and Law." Scout Oath: "On my honor I will do my best to do my duty to God and my country and to obey the Scout Law; to help other people at all times; to keep myself physically strong, mentally awake, and morally straight." Scout Law: "A Scout is: Trustworthy, Loyal, Helpful, Friendly, Courteous, Kind, Obedient, Cheerful, Thrifty, Brave, Clean, Reverent" (Boy Scouts of America National Council, http://www.scouting.org/nav/enter. jsp?s=mc&c=mv).

6. C. S. Lewis, *Mere Christianity* (New York: Macmillan, 1952), 102.

7. Cara Mia DiMassa, "Being a CEO 'in the Tradition of Abraham,'" *Los Angeles Times*, November 10, 2002.

8. C. S. Lewis, *The Screwtape Letters* (San Francisco: Harper Collins, 1996), 1.

9. Francis De Sales, *Introduction to the Devout Life*, trans. and ed. John K. Ryan (New York: Doubleday, 1989), 153.

10. Frank C. Laubach, *Man of Prayer* (Syracuse, NY: New Readers Press, 1990), 193–194.

11. Laubach, 27.

CHAPTER 6

1. William Law, *A Serious Call to a Devout and Holy Life* (New York: Paulist Press, 1978), 78.

2. Taken from *Hearing God* by Dallas Willard. Copyright© 1984, 1993, 1999 by Dallas Willard. Used with permission of InterVarsity Press, PO Box 1400, Downers Grove, IL 60515. ivpress.com.

3. Jan Johnson, *When the Soul Listens* (Colorado Springs, CO:

NavPress, 1999), 125.

4. F. B. Meyer, *The Secret of Guidance* (Chicago: Moody Press, 1997), 18.

5. Willard, *Hearing God*, 168.

6. Willard, *Hearing God*, 31.

7. Oswald Chambers, *My Utmost for His Highest* (Uhrichsville, OH: Barbour, 1963), entries for October 30 and 31.

8. Frank C. Laubach, *Man of Prayer* (Syracuse, NY: New Readers Press, 1963), 23.

9. Elizabeth Rooney, "Opening," *A Widening Light: Poems of the Incarnation*, ed. Luci Shaw (Vancouver, British Columbia: Regent College Publishing, 2000), 117.

CHAPTER 7

1. These elements come directly from the talk "How God Is in Business" by Dallas Willard (see appendix A).

2. I would recommend *Boundaries* (Grand Rapids, MI: Zondervan, 1992) by Dr. Henry Cloud and Dr. John Townsend for a more detailed treatment on this subject.

3. William Law, *A Serious Call to a Devout and Holy Life* (New York: Paulist Press, 1978), 75.

4. Law, 58.

APPENDIX A

1. This was a talk to a gathering of business people in Macon, Georgia, on August 8, 2001. No notes from that talk were available. For ease of reading, this talk has been modified by the author and Dallas Willard for readability and understanding. These changes were made in keeping with the ideas and intentions expressed by the speaker.

2. The nature and purpose of work are two key ideas about work. This statement is a "nature" statement about work and reflects its essence or character and power.

3. This is one of the great "humiliations" of work as we experience it today—the filling of our jobs with tasks, duties, and concerns that have little or nothing to do with our actual job. The $500 hammer on the space shuttle was a classic example of waste in industry, but in reality it did cost $500 to comply with and document all the federal regulations for that hammer.

4. From Socrates and the ancient Greeks to our founding fathers, the possession of moral knowledge was considered utterly crucial for the survival of individuals and societies. "The life of the nation is secure only while the nation is honest, truthful, and virtuous." —Fredrick Douglass. We have lost our way in this area, and we are at risk. Calvin Coolidge wrote, "The foundations of our society and our government rest so much on the teachings of the Bible that it would be difficult to support them if faith in these teachings would cease to be practically universal in our country." We are close to that point, and we have nothing capable of supporting those foundations should we reach it.

5. William James quoted in William Carl Rudiger *The Principles of Education* (New York: Houghton Mifflin, 1910), 275.

6. The circle diagram of job, ministry, work, life is a key chapter in the book. Just being able to think about my life in that way and to think about how to honor each and bring God into each was a freedom I had never known.

7. Antonio Machado, "The Wind, One Brilliant Day," in trans. Robert Bly, *The Winged Energy of Delight* (New York: HarperCollins, 2004), 69.

APPENDIX B

1. John Ruskin, "Unto This Last," *Unto This Last & Other Essays on Art and Political Economy.* (London: J. M. Dent and Sons, 1907), 128–131. This piece was recommended by Dallas Willard as a window into advanced moral thought on the value of work and the potential nobility of the merchant.

APPENDIX C

1. Louis D. Brandeis, *Business: A Profession* (Boston: Small, Maynard & Company, 1914), 1–12. Another excerpt suggested by Dallas Willard to "help the reader think about important matters."

ABOUT THE AUTHOR

BILL HEATLEY serves on the board of directors for the Theology of Work Project, a collective that researches employment issues and concerns through a Christian worldview. Bill and his family reside in Oak Park, California. For more information, visit www.theologyofwork.org.

Check out these other great titles!

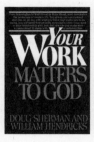

Your Work Matters to God
Doug Sherman and William Hendricks
ISBN-13: 978-0-89109-372-5
ISBN-10: 0-89109-372-9

Are you unclear on the value of secular work? What is your view of everyday work? Are you pleased with your job, or do you suspect God would prefer you in some type of "full-time Christian service"? Let this book help you explore these questions and more!

Handbook for Personal Bible Study
Dr. William W. Klein
ISBN-13: 978-1-60006-117-2
ISBN-10: 1-60006-117-6

Author Bill Klein delivers a unique handbook for getting the most out of studying Scripture, using a wealth of references to cover relevant topics in a simple, easy-to-use format. You'll find everything you need to make the most of your time spent in God's Word.

To order copies, visit your local Christian bookstore, call NavPress at 1-800-366-7788, or log on to www.navpress.com.
To locate a Christian bookstore near you, call 1-800-991-7747.